OLD TESTAMENT TEMPLATE

**Rediscovering God's Principles
for Discipling all Nations**

Landa L. Cope

The Old Testament Template - Rediscovering God's Principles for
Discipling Nations

Publisher: The Template Institute Press, Burtigny, Switzerland

ISBN-10 2-8399-0124-2
ISBN-13 978-2-8399-0124-6

Printed in Belarus.
Printcorp. LP # 02330/0056863 of 30.04.04. Ord. 408 (06007 A). Qty 20 000 cps.

The Template Institute Press is the publishing arm of The Template Institute.

The Template Institute exists to create, produce and multiply materials and seminars that
teach the biblical template and promote biblical thinking in the workplace and on issues
of concern to communities and nations.

Sales and distribution from:

The Template Institute Press
1268 Burtigny
Switzerland

E-mail: info@templateinstitute.com
Internet: www.templateinstitute.com
Phone: +41 (0)22 366 02 10

To my mom who, with all her highs and lows, never wavered from her love and commitment to the truth and power of the Word of God. The desperate prayers of a loving mother are not wasted.

Margaret Adeline Kelley Cope 1912 to 2002

There are so many people to thank that I am sure I will unintentionally miss some. Please forgive me. Any work we produce is really the sum total of all that others have given us and the grace of God to help us use it.

I am grateful to Loren Cunningham and Tom Marshall for sparking a burning passion for God's Kingdom truth in my heart. Joy Dawson, Campbell McAlpine and Gordon Olsen modeled careful, methodical passion for the Word of God as a foundation for everything we do. Michael Cassidy was and is my hero who has let his heart be broken with the lost truths of God and the impact this has had on our nations. Gunnar Olson listened to a cassette of the first message and opened up doors for me to share Christ around the world. And there are scores of pastors and biblical scholars all over the world who have assured me that I was not crazy and that this message must get out.

On the working team I need to mention the Omaha ladies edit team who got me through the first draft; my P.A. Erin Pennington, and Jenni Lotz and Olivia Jackson who looked up loads of facts; John Darnall, Chris Ruzin, and Cameron Thorp got us through the artwork, web page and logo design; Erin Pennington and Tove Poulsen who gave the energy and commitment to push through the last drafts; and, of course, Lucile Allen who made it all so much more readable with her final editing.

Many thanks go to ten years of Advanced Principles of Communications students who helped hammer out the ideas and multiply the message. I could not have continued without your steady encouragement that this was life-changing stuff. And the same with the thousands of people who have attended seminars around the world and given feedback. Larry Wright and his team at Procla Media caught the vision very early on and produced a really good video series that has, and is, blessing thousands with this material before it was written down.

To my dear friends Fiona, Colleen, Matt, Tove and my P.A. Erin Pennington for believing in the material as much as I do and never letting me forget that God is near. And to my team at Burtigny who have given me so much grace and encouragement to do this work while they carried other weights in my absence.

Finally, and always, my thanks to God who lets me continue to enter into the ecstasy of knowing Him and talking about Him all over the world.

CONTENTS
The Old Testament Template

November 2005

In a small cabin on the western slopes of Colorado in August of 1975, our family of four was taking a holiday week. On the second day I received in prayer from the Lord seven "spheres of society" to be used strategically to disciple nations (Matthew 28:18-20). I wrote them on a yellow legal pad: Family (home); Church (religion); Education, Media (electronic and printed); Celebration (arts, entertainment and sports); Economy (research and development, production, sales and service, i.e., commerce) and Government (all branches).

The next day my wife, Darlene, and I were invited to meet with Bill and Vonnette Bright, founders of Campus Crusade for Christ, as they too were in Colorado. As we visited, I was reaching into my coat pocket for my list when Bill announced to us that God had shown him the strategy for discipling a nation! I looked at his list, and they included the same areas.

This is not new, but a renewed revelation. In the 19th Century, Abraham Kyper of Holland had a list of four "jurisdictions" from God through His Word. William Carey, a London shoe cobbler who became a pioneer missionary in India, launched programs in all seven spheres of society. He published the first periodical in all of Asia, founded a lending bank for the poor, started schools, planted churches, and helped change laws to stop widow burning, to name a few.

The truths of God's Word remain true in all centuries. The transformation of nations through transformed followers of Jesus can and will happen in this, the 21st Century, as we apply His truth in and through our lives.

Heads of state, corporation CEOs, church leaders, and leaders of virtually all spheres of society have been impacted and encouraged by Landa Cope's presentation of God's template for transforming nations. Although she arranges the spheres a little differently than I do, the principles and strategy are the same.

I'm happy that Landa, a friend of more than three decades, has put this powerful truth into writing. Read and be challenged, and changed.

Loren Cunningham
Kailua-Kona, Hawaii

Landa Cope is both a prophetess and an Esther for such a time as this. Of all the speakers and leaders I have known around the world over the last couple of decades, no one quite matches Landa for her passion to see nations discover the divine pattern of living for their national lives. Some people think *individual,* yet others think *local church,* but Landa thinks *nation.* In fact, she thinks the world. But she sees the world through the lens of God's purposes for the multiple nations of the world.

And because there are so few Christian leaders in the world who deeply think nationally, Landa has special significance and this book is of particular importance, especially for Christian leaders whether they operate from a local church, para-church or denominational base.

In this volume Landa is challenging all of us to think afresh about what sort of God we really have. Is He simply concerned with the things of Heaven and how to get His sinful earthlings there? Of course, that is major in the divine intention, and no one knows that better than Landa. But she has also profoundly grasped God's Old Testament word: "I am the Lord who practices steadfast love, justice, and righteousness *in the earth;* for in these things I delight, says the Lord" (Jeremiah 9:24). This scripture gives us the breathtaking affirmation that not only is the Lord Himself a God of unswerving love, justice and righteousness, this being His fundamental character, but He actually *practices* them.

He works them out in deeds. That is the kind of God He is. That is His character. He is an active, working, functioning God, caught up in certain divine deeds and practice. But now, fasten your seat belts for the next bit – and this is what Landa has grasped way better than most people I know – this God works out His characteristics and practices them not simply in Heaven but on earth. This ties in with Jesus' instruction to us to pray for the Kingdom to come and for His will to be done on earth (Matthew 6:10) as it is in Heaven. And it also fits in with both the Psalmist and St Paul's reminder to us that "the earth is the Lord's" (Psalm 24:1; 1 Corinthians 10:26). So the earth is God's special arena for practicing and working out His love, justice, and righteousness.

And the arena most specifically through which this is meant to be worked out is in individual nations. Landa's powerful and prophetic volume is therefore a passionate appeal to the Lord's people to join in the study and search for God's nation-building values. My prayer is that this book will be used and read widely and that we will catch something of Landa's panoramic vision, be challenged by some of her encyclopaedic grasp of this theme, and be volitionally motivated into discovering afresh the real biblical strategies needed under God to bring changes He wants to see in His world.

Absorbing this volume will put a bomb under our seats and catapult us out into the world with new insight, energy, wisdom and effective transformational ministries.

If you are ready and have the stomach and heart for such a challenge, read on. But if you are overly devoted to the armchair, then put this book on one side, relax back into your comfort zone, and miss out on one of the greatest adventures life and eternity can offer. Because winning and truly discipling the nations is just that kind of adventure.

Michael Cassidy
South Africa

I am sitting in a small guesthouse in Potchefstroom, South Africa. Last night, and the two nights before, I spoke to a thousand South African university students about the call of God on each of their lives to bless and develop their nation. As I worshiped with them, and it was powerful worship, I was reminded of the summer of 1972 at the Munich Olympics. A thousand young people gathered in a tent just outside the city. We were there for the first-ever Olympic outreach and we were there to change our world. Joy Dawson spoke on "God Is Always Greater."

From that one outreach and Youth With a Mission's one base in Lausanne, Switzerland, our mission exploded to over a thousand bases in 150 countries and hundreds of outreaches all over the world with millions of young people involved over the next 33 years. YWAM, OM, Campus Crusade and other Spirit-lead youth missions launched what missiologists now refer to as the third wave of missions. Faithful, amazing God!

Now it is time for the fourth wave! It is time for the largest church in history to become the deepest church in history. Last night, speaking to those South African students, I saw the face of the future. Pray with me for the release of this new generation of world-changers. Pray with me for a global revolution of political and economic justice, revival of the church and explosion of wholeness in individuals and families. Pray with me that God's glory will be seen – and that every Christian worldwide will follow Saint Francis of Assisi's admonition to be a witness all day, everyday and, when necessary, use words.

God never changes. Pray that we, His people, do.

Landa Lea Cope
Potchefstroom, South Africa
August 17, 2005

PART I

OLD TESTAMENT
TEMPLATE

THE JOURNEY

This book is dedicated to the study of what the Bible has to say about all of life including government, family, the arts, education, science, communication, economics, and the role of the church. We want to rediscover a faith that influences our thinking and actions in every arena of living.

In history, Christians have thought and acted in ways that influenced the communities and nations in which they lived. Much of that influence was positive, affecting things like the development of public education, workers' rights, economic development, the concept of a free press, help for the victimized and disenfranchised. We believe that this kind of influence is lacking in Christian life today, and we would like to discover why.

Martin Luther is noted as having said that a gospel that does not deal with the issues of the day is not the Gospel at all. We want to discover the biblical thinking that will address the issues of the 21st Century in an effective and redemptive way. There is a reason the Christian faith has become weak and ineffectual in dealing with issues of politics, economics, beauty, the family, and daily issues of life. We want to discover what has gone wrong, but more importantly, we want to rediscover the biblical basis that led generations of believers to influence their times.

We are searching, and we invite you to join the search. I have put the challenge of these questions on every continent of the world to presidents, members of cabinets, leaders in politics, business, and church. It seems to be striking a chord of need. In order to facilitate getting the message out and bringing multinational, multicultural thinking and faith to the process, we have begun this work.

Our goal is to help bring vital relevant, effective Christian thought and action back into the 21st Century. We are on a journey with more questions than answers; we invite your companionship and contribution.

CHAPTER 1
What's Wrong With This Picture?

"Do you have eyes but fail to see, and ears but fail to hear?"

Mark 8:18

"Once more Jesus put his hands on the man's eyes. Then his eyes were opened, his sight was restored, and he saw everything clearly."

Mark 8:25

I was mindlessly channel surfing through scores of TV programs to pass the time. I landed on a British journalist who was saying that Christians believe that many of them living in a community will affect that community for good. The greater the Christian presence, the greater the benefit to the society at large. I agreed with the commentator; that is what we teach.

He went on to propose that we look at the most Christianized city in America to see how this influence works out practically. He defined "Christianized" as the community with the largest percentage of believers actually attending church regularly. This is a good conservative working definition of Christianized.

By that definition, then, Dallas, Texas was the most Christianized city in America at that time. More people per capita were in church on any given Sunday than any other community in the country. Churches abound in Dallas and a large number boast full pews. Our journalist proposed that we look at the social demographics of Dallas to see how this "Christian blessing" worked out practically within that community.

We looked at various statistics and studies, including crime, safety on the streets, police enforcement, and the justice and penal system. We looked at health care, hospitals, emergency care, contagious diseases, infant mortality rate, and the distribution of care-givers. We reviewed education, equality of schools, safety, test scores and graduation statistics. Jobs, housing, and general economics were evaluated. Can you get a job? Can you get housing? Does potential income match available housing? We looked at homelessness and programs for those unable to care for themselves. Is there equality regardless of color, creed or income? And so on. Each of these categories was evaluated using racial and economic factors.

The TV host looked at the statistics and information you would be concerned about if you were going to raise your children in a community. Will my children be safe on the streets? Can they get a respectable, safe education? Will I be able to house, clothe and feed my family? Will my children have blatant exposure to drugs and other destructive influences? Can my family be relatively safe from disease? Is adequate medical attention available if they get sick? Can I get legal help and a fair hand from the judicial system? Are the police equally interested in our protection, and is all of this true regardless of my color, nationality or creed?

The program was, perhaps, an hour long and I watched it alone. By the time my English host was done with the Dallas study I was devastated. No one would want to live in a city in that condition. The crime, the decrepit social systems, the disease, the economic discrepancies, the racial injustice all disqualified this community from having an adequate quality of life. And this was the "most Christianized" city in America. I wanted to weep.

The program was not finished. The host took this devastating picture of a broken community to the Christian leaders and asked for their observations. He chose leaders of status and integrity. He chose the kind of Christian leaders other Christians would respect. One by one, each pastor viewed the same facts that I had just seen about the condition of his city. With simplicity, the narrator asked each minister, "As a Christian leader, what is your response to the condition of your community?" Without exception, in various ways, they all said the same thing, "This is not my concern...I'm a spiritual leader."

The program finished, the room was silent, and my world began to crumble. Many years of my work as a missionary have been spent addressing Christianity's critics, specifically those in the media. (This is not generally very difficult as their accusations are often ill-informed or poorly-formulated.) If this journalist had turned the microphone to me for comment at the closing of his program I would have been speechless. I was shocked to silence...by the facts.

I had no argument against the case this journalist had built. As Christians, we do say our faith, lived out, will influence a society toward good. We go beyond this. I have heard it said, and have taught, that it only takes twenty percent of a society believing anything to influence, even lead, the other eighty percent in a given direction. We teach that the gospel is good for a society, that its values will bless those beyond the members of faith. But the facts about Dallas do not support this notion. We must look at the facts! Dallas has considerably more than twenty percent professing Christians. Can we say that this city is the legacy of Christian influence?

I was reeling with implications and questions. Why had I not been honest enough to see the discrepancy between my teaching and the visible results? Why had it taken a non-Christian to point these things out to me? How could we, as Christian leaders, say "quality of life" issues are not our concern? If the Gospel does influence all of society, how could America, with more Christians per capita, possibly, than any other time in its history, be slipping from biblical values in virtually every arena? Slipping in crime, immorality, poverty, corruption, justice, disease, drugs, homelessness, literacy and more? How was it that I, and the myriad committed Christians I know, had never put this all together? Why had we not judged ourselves...and found ourselves wanting?

Search For Truth

I came to Christianity reluctantly. As a college student I was a committed atheist and gave speeches on why not to believe in the Bible. I longed for truth, practical truth, that could be lived on a daily basis. I hoped for a truth that could lead to justice and genuine love for others. I became a Christian because I became convinced that it was the only belief system that explains the reality of the universe we live in, good and bad. My encounter with that truth, and the person of Jesus Christ, catapulted me into the Kingdom of God. I have spent the years since trying to learn more of the truths of the Kingdom and how to live them out practically and daily in my own life and work. Nevertheless, I have always said that if it could be proven to me that the teachings of the Bible and the life of Christ were not true, I would have to reevaluate everything I believe. Nothing had ever more shaken my confidence in Christianity than this television program. Now my feet were to the fire.

As I battled with the questions this program's revelations demanded, I could see at least three possible answers:

1. God does not exist.
2. God and/or God's Word are not true. The Bible does teach that its values applied will influence society at large, but practically, it does not work.
3. We are not seeing biblical values applied by Christians today, and, therefore, do not see the influence those truths would have and have had in history.

In my heart, I knew that the third option had to be the case. I have never been a Christian for primarily historic, emotional or personal reasons. I am a follower of Christ because I believe the Bible is true and that whenever its teaching and principles are measured and applied they will prove true. My faith was on the line and I believed that the God I knew was up to the challenge. But I needed answers!

Early in my journey with Christ I discovered that some questions are too big for our pitifully limited minds. I learned that these questions are not too great for God. He delights to reveal Himself and lead us to understanding, but He must do the revealing. For overwhelming questions, I have a special shelf in the back of my mind. We are not to throw out the great and crushing questions that challenge our faith and the very nature and character of the One in whom we believe. If we do not face the difficult questions of life and our faith, we lose the opportunity for God to reveal Himself in a greater way. Neither can we wrestle within ourselves with life's most serious dilemmas. We do not have the understanding. We must hold these painful issues before the throne of God until He reveals greater understanding to us. In so doing, we grow in the knowledge of God.

These pressing observations, prompted by the honest analysis of a British journalist, question the validity of what you and I say should be the normal influence that comes with Christianity to a community. What we teach does not seem to match the impact of Christianity today. I put these agonizing questions on the shelf with a prayer. "Father, I believe Your Word and I believe You when You say You want to bless all peoples and use the church to do it. I believe You can bless and that Your principles are true. But, Lord, we do not have the influence we should have in our day. Why Lord? Help me understand, Lord! Help me see!" And He did!

Trip To Africa

I began my overseas life in North Africa, four wonderful years in the land of the pharaohs. I loved Egypt and would gladly have spent my entire life there. More than twenty years later, within months of watching the Dallas documentary, I was on my way to a more expansive exploratory trip of the African continent. For two months I traversed from West to East to Southern Africa: Togo, Ghana, Nigeria, Kenya, Uganda, and South Africa. Africa is enormous and I spent hours in airplanes looking down on its vastness.

The "Dallas questions" still sat on my mental back shelf. How could a Christian community be in such abominable shape? How could the gospel result in such chaos? As I visited primarily Christianized nations, Togo, Ghana, Nigeria, Kenya and Uganda, my anguish increased. Missions statistics that I had quoted with joy burned in my mind. "Africa, eighty percent Christian south of the Sahara by the end of this century." "Africa, the most evangelized continent in the world." "Africa, the most churched continent by the end of this century."

In each nation, the story was the same: poverty, disease, violence, corruption, injustice and chaos met me at every turn. I found myself asking: "Is this Thy Kingdom come, Thy will be done on earth as it is in heaven?" Is this what the blessing of the gospel brought into a community looks like? Is this what a nation looks like when it is "reached"? In this southern part of Africa we have nearly reached every "creature." Churches are planted and full. African evangelists abound and continue the work. Is this what it looks like when our work as Christians is finished in a nation? God forbid! My anguish increased.

You may say, "This is unfair. These were poor countries before the gospel came!" You are right, but some are poorer and more diseased now, *after* the gospel has come.[1] I spent many hours asking God how this could be. How could we, as Christians and especially missionaries, be patting our backs for a job well done in Southern and Central Africa? How could we speak so glowingly of the gospel's great reformation of Europe and North America and not see that none of that nation-changing reality is being experienced in Africa? How could anyone conceive of this utterly devastated Africa as finished? How could anyone believe that Africa or deteriorating Dallas, for that matter, are examples of the impact of Christianity? How could we hold up the condition of the so-called Christianized nations today as trophies of the truth, as proof that where the gospel of Jesus Christ is spread, blessing accompanies it?

My heart was heavy as I traveled Africa, as I thought about my own nation. My prayer became, "Lord, what has gone wrong?" Nearly two hundred years of concentrated missions effort on this continent – how could it result in this? With a dawning revelation that would change my understanding of missions and my life calling, God spoke simply, fundamentally, and permanently. "The devastation you see is the fruit of preaching salvation alone, without the rest of the biblical message."

---

1. *Kinoti, George "Hope for Africa" and "What The Christian Can Do". Nairobi: AISRED, 1994*

CHAPTER 2
We've Lost Our Christian Minds

"Jesus replied: 'Love the Lord your God with all your heart and with all your soul and with all your mind.' This is the first and the greatest commandment."

Matthew 22:37-38

"For if I pray in a tongue, my spirit prays, but my mind is unfruitful. So what shall I do? I will pray with my spirit, but I will also pray with my mind..."

I Corinthians 14:14-15

"The gospel of salvation? What could possibly be the problem with the gospel of salvation?" you may ask. The answer to that? Nothing! There is nothing wrong with the *salvation* part of the gospel message we preach today. But as evangelicals, we talk about the *salvation message,* being *born again, born again believers, born again churches, the new birth, Jesus saves,* as though the initial experience of salvation is the *only* message. Jesus preached that the only way to enter the kingdom of heaven is through Himself, but He constantly put salvation in the context of the broader message of the kingdom of heaven. He never referred to the *gospel of salvation.* Jesus taught the gospel of the Kingdom: salvation and the truth about every dimension of life. Yet, more than 150 years of mission work has been dominated by this concept of salvation as our singular goal.

The result of this truncated gospel message is no less tragic than a grown child still incapable of doing anything for himself. Something has gone terribly wrong. God's design has been interrupted, and this life has not fully developed. The child is still precious and a great gift of life, but God's original plans and purposes for that infant have been distorted. That principle is the same in all of His Kingdom. We are not only to be born again; we are to grow up into the things of God as they apply to all of life. We are meant to have our minds transformed and every thought taken captive with the truths of God's great Kingdom. We are to know how God wants us to live!

In what Michael Cassidy of South Africa, calls "the Great Reversal,"[1] we have taken the holistic message preached in the Old and New Testaments and reduced our message to the entry point into the Kingdom. The beginning has become the goal: salvation! We want to "get people saved." When we get them saved, we want to "get them in church!" We then move on to reach those who have never heard. This is our concept of missions; this is evangelism. When a people has heard our gospel of salvation and the church is planted, we begin to feel we have finished our job. Two, three, five hundred years ago, the church fathers would have found this emphasis on salvation, to the exclusion of the rest of the message, astounding. The message that reformed Western cultures and built nations on solidly Christian values was not the *gospel of salvation,* but the *gospel of the Kingdom* – including salvation.

The truths of the gospel of the Kingdom, are to transform us as they teach us how to live every part of life. Our transformed lives are then to be salt and light to our families, neighborhoods, communities, and, finally, our nations, making them *better* places to live for everyone. Not perfect communities, not heaven on earth, but better because the influence of good is as great, if not greater, than evil. There have been great examples of this in history. Transforming lives has been so emphasized in church history that it's been said that *never* has a revivalist lived who believed God's purpose ended with revival. They all believed true revival culminated in significant reformation of communities through a revived church's influence on society at large.

The first church transformed Israel, revolutionized the Roman Empire, and laid foundations for Western European countries to become the most prosperous nations in the world. What a different impact we see in modern mission history. Evangelized Africa is worse today in every arena – disease,

---

1. *Cassidy, Michael "The Passing Summer".* Hotter S. Stoughton, London

crime, justice, economics, and the family – than before Christianity came to the continent.[2] America has a huge and apparently increasing percentage of practicing believers and, yet, it also is decreasing in moral fiber and quality of life in every category. Missionary workers in the sub-continent of India say that, while we quote that Nagaland is eighty percent Christianized, we fail to note that seventy percent of the teenagers in the capital city are drug addicts. Rwanda, with some sixty years of on-going revival in the church, suffers genocide in tribal civil war. Some say that there are more Christians alive today than the sum total of Christians in history. Where is the power to influence and transform communities that the Apostle Paul, St. Patrick, Calvin and many others experienced in their day?

Does the fruit of modern evangelism today reflect "…thy Kingdom come, thy will be done on earth as it in heaven…"? Surely not! So, where have we gone wrong? How did we come to such a reduced gospel? The good news is that there is an answer to that question. It is good news because the first step to change is knowing where the problem lies. In this case, one problem is that we have lost our Christian minds!

The Split Christian Mind

Over the last two centuries Christians, especially evangelicals, have developed a split view of the world. This process has taken place at different times, in different regions of the world, and in differing denominations, but we can generally say that split thinking dominates much of Christianity today.

Recent dualistic thinking developed like this: one part of the church took the stand that God takes care of salvation and, therefore, it is the church's responsibility to look after man's more basic needs such as food, clothing, shelter, health, and perhaps even education. In reaction, another part of the church responded with a resounding, "No!" Its view was that only man's soul and his eternal condition is of any value and our focus is to be the pursuit of man's salvation. The latter thought of themselves as being concerned with *spiritual* matters and the former were considered concerned with *material* matters. Those who saw the church's primary

2. *Kinoti, Ibid*

role as pursuing man's salvation became known as *evangelicals* and they began to refer to the others as *liberals*. Evangelicals were concerned with eternal and heavenly matters. Liberals were more concerned with temporal and earthly issues. Evangelicals preached the *spiritual* gospel of salvation and were focused on the sacred issues of life. Liberals, evangelicals thought, preached the *social* gospel and were more concerned with *secular* issues of life. This split view of the world was exaggerated by an increasing emphasis on the immediate return of Christ and the concept that everything *secular* was going to hell.

This is a very basic way of looking at considerably more complex doctrinal issues. I am neither a theologian nor an historian, and I am not attempting to deal with these broader issues. My point here is simply that a split view of the world entered the thinking of the church, and this dualistic view systematically reduced the primary message of the gospel preached today to salvation alone. Christians, in the main, became more concerned about the invisible issues of the faith: salvation, prayer, spiritual warfare, heaven and healing. We began to believe we only had time to get souls saved.

THE SPLIT GOSPEL

SPIRITUAL	**MATERIAL**
SALVATION	**SOCIAL**
ETERNAL	**TEMPORAL**
HEAVENLY	**EARTHLY**
EVANGELICAL	**LIBERAL**
SACRED	**SECULAR**

The tragedy in this division, as is so often the case, is that both sides were right and both sides were wrong. Evangelicals were right about what the gospel *was* concerned with, and wrong in what they felt was *not* the gospel's concern. The gospel of the Kingdom that Jesus taught, built on the entire teaching of God to Israel through Moses and the prophets, was a message that dealt with sin and salvation, with heaven and hell, with prayer and spiritual warfare. The liberals were accurate in that it was also a message of God's desire for justice in government, equity in economics, the righteous use of science and technology, communication, family, the arts, and all of life.

The result of a diminished and split gospel is clear in the world we live in today. Never have there been more Christians, in more churches, in more nations, speaking more languages of the world. But I think it would also be fair to say that never has the spread of the church had less impact on surrounding communities. The Christian church today is a huge church and a weak church because we have lost most of the gospel message. We can say that the social, economic, and judicial issues of our communities are not our concern because we have a split view of the world. We are "spiritual leaders" and do not need to concern ourselves with secular matters. We do not need to stop bringing the message of salvation, but we desperately need to regain the essential truths of the rest of the gospel message of God's Kingdom. We need to renew our Christian minds and see our lives transformed by conforming every thought to the thinking of Christ. Then the 21st Century church will turn our world upside down. Then the body of Christ will not only be large and diverse, it will regain its power of influence.

CHAPTER 3
We've Lost Our Mission

"For if he lays the foundation and is not able to finish it, everyone who sees it will ridicule him, saying, 'This fellow began to build and was not able to finish.'"

Luke 14:29-30

"Perseverance must finish its work so that you may be mature and complete, not lacking anything."

Luke 1:4

A friend taught me the very important lesson, when given a new job to do, of always asking, "What does a job well done look like?" You cannot possibly do well what you do not understand. If the church is to do what Christ has left us here to do, we must know what our job is and what it's to look like when we have finished.

Towards the end of His life Jesus prayed this prayer, "(Father,) I have brought you glory on earth by completing the work you gave me to do."[1] His Father had sent Him into time and space to accomplish specific objectives. He knew what they were, and He completed them. The entire work of reaching the world was not accomplished at his death, but Jesus understood that He was not sent to do everything. Much of the Father's mission would be carried on and completed by the church He would leave behind. But, for the time being, His specific role as Son and Messiah was complete.

After nearly thirty years in missions, I marvel at this text. So often as Christian workers we do not even know what our job is. If something

---

1. *John 17:4*

needs to be done, it must be our responsibility to do it. I don't remember ever hearing a minister say, "I completed my work." Jesus, however, did not think that *everything* was His responsibility. He knew what the Father had sent Him to do, and He knew when he had completed it. We can learn much from this in our own lives and callings. Do you know what God has called you to do?

Another thing that strikes me from this text is that the Father was glorified by Jesus finishing His job. When I am introduced as a speaker, my hosts often string together a long list of accomplishments from my life. They are trying to give the audience a point of reference and reasons why they might want to listen to me. While that is much appreciated, it is so important that I not become impressed with my own P.R. God is not looking at the past; He is looking at the finish. He is challenging me to not only begin well, but to finish well. Then, and only then, will He be glorified in my life and through my work for Him. On a personal level, these are sobering challenges and good questions to raise in prayer on a regular basis. Are you doing what God called you to do? Will you finish it?

What Is "The Work" Of The Church?

Beyond this personal lesson, we can also apply these questions to the institution of the church. What is the work of the church? How do we know if we have finished it? How do we evaluate and measure a generation's obedience as the body of Christ? What are our specific goals and how do we develop strategies and evaluate their value? Answering these questions is key to transforming a huge church into an influential church in the 21st Century. Historically, some have said our work is to get people saved and to build the church globally. Others have said we are to be more concerned with man's material needs such as food, shelter, and protection. But what does God say? What does the Bible teach as the mandate for our existence on this planet? If we know what God's Word says, we can build our future on solid foundations.

The Golden Thread Of Purpose: Reach and Teach

At the end of His life on earth Jesus gives instructions to His disciples. This is their record of what He said:

Matthew 28:18-19
Then Jesus came to them and said, "All authority in heaven and on earth has been given to Me. Therefore go and make disciples of all nations, baptizing them in the name of the Father and of the Son and of the Holy Spirit, and teaching them to obey everything I have commanded you. And surely I am with you always, to the very end of the age."

Mark 16:15
He said to them, "Go into all the world and preach the good news to all creation."

Luke 24:45-47
Then he opened their minds so they could understand the Scriptures. He told them, "This is what is written: The Christ will suffer and rise from the dead on the third day, and repentance and forgiveness of sins will be preached in His name to all nations, beginning at Jerusalem.

Many have reduced these objectives to two simple mandates saying that Christ has called us to "reach every creature" and to "disciple all nations." This would fit with what seems to be God's emphasis throughout the Bible for man's very existence.

There is a continuity from Adam to Christ... a golden thread of purpose for our existence. To Adam and Eve, male and female, God speaks these words:

Genesis 1:28
God blessed them and said to them, 'Be fruitful and increase in number; fill the earth and subdue it. Rule over the fish of the sea and the birds of the air and over every living creature that moves on the ground.'

To Abraham and his descendants God spoke time and again, saying things like this:

Genesis 22:17-18
I will surely bless you and make your descendants as numerous as the stars in the sky and as the sand on the seashore. Your descendants will take possession of the cities of their enemies, and through your offspring all nations on earth will be blessed, because you have obeyed me.

It seems clear that this multiplying and blessing emphasis, the quantitative and qualitative approach, are in God's purpose and plan for man from His creation. We are here to fill the earth and steward it to God's glory. This purposed statement did not disappear or dissipate with the fall of man and the coming of sin, although sin would now have to be dealt with.

We can look at the work of the church in two dimensions – the breadth aspect of reaching every creature, and the depth aspect of blessing and discipling all nations. Of these two areas, we have understood the growth dimension of our job really well in the last two centuries.

The Quantitative Task: Reaching Every Creature

The quantitative task of the church can be measured, mapped, and graphed. This has been, perhaps, the most exciting century in church history for globally measuring and targeting the unreached. We have amazing amounts of information to help us evaluate our job of reaching. Whole organizations have been formed in the last 30 years solely committed to tracking and documenting how we are doing as a generation of Christians in fulfilling our mandate to reach every person on earth with the Gospel.

We know that there are nearly six billion people on the planet today. We know that more than ninety percent of those who have never heard the Gospel live in what missions call the 10/40 window. This window lies between the 10th and the 40th latitude from West Africa across all of Asia. Within this window lies most of the Muslim, Buddhist, Hindu, and

Confucian world. We know that fewer than five percent of the world's Christian missionaries work inside of that 10/40 window and the remaining ninety-five percent or more work where less than ten percent have never heard the claims of Christ. This gives us a very clear picture of where we are to pour our energies if we are going to complete the task of reaching every creature in our generation.

In addition to our awareness of the population and geographic challenges of this task, we know today that some 11,000 languages in the world still have no witness of Jesus. We know which of these groups have already been targeted by translation ministries and how long it will take them to be reached. Computers, language, and mapping programs have made this an exciting area of research giving meaningful tools to workers in the field. All of it helps us to evaluate the job the church needs to accomplish and the strategies needed to do it.

We can compare the job of reaching every creature today with the job for the first generation church. We know that in Paul's day approximately one church existed for every 400 or more people groups that needed to be reached with the gospel. Today more than 400 churches exist for each unreached tribe. In the first generation church, one Christian believed we were to reach the world for every seven who needed to hear. Today there are seven Christians for every person who has never heard the Gospel. Yes, more people live on the planet today than in all prior human history, but more Christians and more churches are trying to reach them than at any point in human history. The quantitative task of "reaching every creature" in this generation is advancing. We can be proud of the church's commitment to this in our age. The work must continue and increase, of course. Our job is to finish, to reach every creature, if God is to be glorified in our generation.

But what about teaching, blessing, discipling all nations? What does this job mean and are we doing it?

The Qualitative Task: Discipling All Nations

Along with telling the disciples to reach every creature, Jesus, at the end of His life, re-emphasized man's second mandate. He tells them to "make disciples of all nations." God's destiny for man, for Israel, for nations, and finally for the church was never size alone. He was concerned with our quality of life. If reaching individuals is the quantitative task, then discipling them and their communities is the qualitative work of teaching and applying truth to life-producing growth and maturity.

What does it mean to disciple a nation? What does a discipled nation look like? These are difficult questions, difficult because qualitative evaluations are harder to make. When is a person mature? When is an act great? How do you determine when an economy is developed? What is poor? What makes a painting good? These questions are even harder in this age because for the last one to two hundred years we have been focusing almost solely on the quantitative growth of the church. The result is that we have perhaps the largest church in history – and the shallowest.

We may not know what it means to disciple a nation, but surely we know what it does *not* mean. When we look at Dallas, Texas or Malawi or Rwanda or any other Christianized community or country today are we willing to say, "This is what it looks like when we are finished"? Is this God's will done on earth as it is in heaven? Surely not!

If we are to glorify the Father in our generation we must know what our job is, and do it. We are reaching the unreached, but those reached individuals, communities, and nations are living in unacceptable conditions. Dr. George Kinoti of Kenya says, "The wretchedness of the African people dishonors their Creator. Therefore, every Christian has a moral responsibility to do his or her very best to correct the situation."[2]

It is not enough to reach the unreached. It is not enough to plant churches amongst those who have no churches. We are to disciple individuals, and through them, disciple their communities and nations. If we do not, we are not fulfilling the purpose for which we were created and given eternal life. Moreover, if we do not disciple the nations, God is not glorified in our generation. He is glorified when we *finish* the work He has left for us to do. Saving souls and planting churches is a beginning. But the quality of those churches and the impact of the lives of the believers on their communities is the litmus test of the quality of our work for Christ. Right now we are failing to do our job well. Christian pollster George Barna finds there is "no significant difference"

---

2. Kinoti, Ibid

between the behavior of people in the United States who call themselves born-again Christian and those who do not make that claim. Muslim evangelists in Africa ask, "What does Christianity do for the people?" The answer today is *nothing*. Nothing changes. The churches get bigger. More and more people get saved. But nothing changes. They are still poor, diseased, uneducated, and left in political and economic chaos.

We must grieve, weep, and mourn this state of affairs in the church today, as Nehemiah did over the condition of Jerusalem.[3] We need to fast and pray because the body of Christ and our communities world-wide are in "great trouble and disgrace." We need to rise up, put on the mind of Christ, and become all He intended the church to be.

The question is, "How do we do that?"

---

3. *Nehemiah 1:3*

CHAPTER 4
The Corn Field Revelation

"Now what I am commanding you today is not too difficult for you or beyond your reach. It is not up in heaven, so that you have to ask, 'Who will ascend into heaven to get it and proclaim it to us so we may obey it?' Nor is it beyond the sea, so that you have to ask, 'Who will cross the seas to get it and proclaim it to us so we may obey it?' No, the word is very near you; it is in your mouth and in your heart so that you may obey it."

Deuteronomy 30:11-14

I was somewhere between Boise, Idaho and Des Moines, Iowa. I can still picture the wheat and cornfields on both sides of the car sliding by, mile after mile. The time of day, the angle of the light, the temperature, the clear blue skies are all as real in my mind at this moment as they were the day God spoke.

For more than a year, it had been clear to me that Christians were missing a significant part of God's revelation. My generation was well on its way to reaching every creature with the salvation message, but had no idea what it meant to disciple nations. How could we regain the wisdom, knowledge, and influence to transform communities with the gospel as the church has done in history? What are the keys? I understood our gospel message was incomplete, but how would we restore the greater revelation?

In my search, I had pursued men and women of God who seemed to see the same deficits in the impact of the church. One man, Tom Marshall, was pastoring a small church in New Zealand. This man of God had an enormous vision of the church's role in building the Kingdom of God and its influence on earth. After he spoke at YWAM's university in Kona, I wept for hours with a broken heart over our diminished gospel message. As I wept, I prayed, "God, You must show us the road back. You must reveal again Your great revelations of Kingdom life beyond salvation." I was so constrained by the Holy Spirit it felt as if I was having a heart attack. "God, You must reveal Yourself to me or I feel I will die of need."

Over the next few days I went to Pastor Marshall and asked the same questions I had put to others. The difference this time was that I was sure Tom Marshall would have the answer. "Tom, how do we do it? How do we actually disciple the nations? How do we put feet to the vision?" His answer was simple, short, and immediate: "I have no idea! God hasn't revealed that to me." That was all he said. To say that I was crestfallen is truly an understatement. The man with the greatest vision in the area of my search had no answers for me. What hope was there?

Within the year I was traveling through the grain fields of the Great Plains states of the U.S.A. I was on a seven-month trip visiting mission bases in America. Driving, for a change, instead of flying, was a great relief for me, and it gave me wonderful time to process and pray. Before I started the journey I had asked the Lord to give me a plan for my time in the car. I had been reading through the Bible nearly every year and a half for over twenty years and had read most of the English versions at least once. During this drive I felt that God gave me a very specific goal of *listening* to the entire Bible from Genesis to Revelation during my trip. I will never forget that morning in the grain fields. The penny dropped and everything in my life, from that moment, changed.

As I was listening to Deuteronomy, suddenly it was as though I was given ears to *hear* what I had read so many times in my life and never understood. I realized the passage I had just listened to was about law! Moses was teaching civil law. Moses was forming government. Then there was a passage on economics; then one on the family and health care; now another on law...and on it went. The light flashed into my poor little brain. Revelation hit like a laser beam. Moses' job was to disciple a nation. His job was to teach a people who had been slaves for more than 300 years how to form and run their nation. Moses was to teach Israel God's principles of government, economics, the family, the priesthood and every God-given domain of human society. He had forty years in the wilderness to do it, and he had written it all down!

What had I been thinking when I read the books of Moses the first twenty or so times? I had been taught to read the scriptures looking for certain themes: salvation, sin, forgiveness, prayer, righteousness, and spiritual warfare. These great themes are there because they are major parts of the gospel message. I had been reading the books allegorically even though it is clear that they are historical records of events that took place in time and space. But, when I read of Israel in bondage to slavery, I saw a message on sin and life without Christ and salvation. When I read about the Jews in the wilderness I learned about the "valley of decision" between the life of sin and God's great promise of salvation. When Israel entered the promise land...salvation! They were God's at last. I preached these messages.

These parallels of sin, decision, and salvation are in the Bible, and there is nothing wrong with teaching them. But, they are not the primary message of the text. What was happening to Moses was real, not allegorical. He had a real population of Jews, in a real desert, with the real challenge of turning them into a prosperous nation. Moses was discipling a real nation in the truths that will make them great in every area of life, and God inspired him to write it all down for you and me. I knew I would never be able to read the Bible in the same way again. My mind was turned upside down.

Moses: What A Job!

What a job Moses had! We think we have needy nations today; look at what he had to deal with! We know that 600,000 able-bodied men left Egypt with Moses.[1] What was the entire population?

If we take the number of women and children for each able-bodied man in Jacob's family of 70[2] when they enter Egypt, it is about 4.5 to 1. At that ratio, the number of Israelites leaving Egypt would have been somewhere around 2,700,000 people. But, remember, they were having problems with the pharaohs because they were multiplying so rapidly

---

1. *Exodus 12:37-38*
2. *Genesis 46:26-27*

they threatened the balance of population with the Egyptians.[3] Further-more, Israel did not leave Egypt alone. Slaves that were not part of Israel left with them as well. They had alien members wandering with them from the very beginning of their wilderness journey. It is no exaggeration to say that Moses was leading more than three million people out of Egypt into the desert.

To put that number in perspective, it amounts to the entire population of New Zealand. The largest refugee situation in modern history was that of the Afghans on the Pakistani border after the invasion by the former Soviet Union. They numbered in the area of two million. Yet, even with the combined resources of the United Nations, the Red Cross, and aid from developed countries, this refugee situation over-whelmed our modern agencies. The Jews had no outside help come to their rescue. Moses' people were in far worse circumstances. The Afghan refugees had a country to go back to. They had homes, schools, businesses, and institutions to which they could return. They had banks, roads, and infrastructures to rebuild even though the Soviet Union had demolished some of them. The Afghans were refugees. The Jews flee-ing Egypt were people without portfolio. They had no country. They had only a promise.

Imagine!

These are a people who have grown from a tribe of seventy people to more than 3,000,000 in 430 years.[4] They have been in exile this entire time. For the last 300 years they have been slave labor under Egyptian pharaohs. They have just walked out of the nation of Egypt with what they are able to carry and the animals they own. Think about it! A U.S. Army Quartermaster General put his mathematical mind to the situation and figured they would require approximately 1,500 tons of food a day – two freight trains worth, each two miles long – and 4,000 tons of firewood to cook the food each day; one million gallons of water daily would be required to drink and wash the dishes. That would necessitate

---

3. *Exodus 1:6-7*
4. *Exodus 12:40*

an 1,800-mile train of tank cars. Their campgrounds would have been two-thirds the size of Rhode Island State. Plus:

- They are poor.
- They have no schools.
- They have no government.
- They have no economy.
- They have no land.
- They have no army.
- They have no industry.
- They have no agriculture.
- They have no religious system.
- They have a welfare mentality and no work ethic.
- They have been oppressed and victimized.
- They have an undeveloped social system.
- They are, without a doubt, the largest, most undeveloped mass of people that has ever existed on the face of the earth. Compared to any nation I can think of today, Israel was in much worse shape.

It is to these people that God says, you are not a people, but I will make you a people. He promises these people, in this condition, that they will become a great nation and that other nations will admire their greatness and be blessed by them.[5] They have just left one of the greatest civilizations in human history, Egypt, in its glory day under the pharaohs. The Jews are an impoverished mob in the middle of a wasteland. Yet, to them God says He will make them a great nation! Can you imagine the unbelief, the bewilderment, even the cynicism they might have felt?

However, in about 300 years' time, God does it. He makes them one of the greatest, if not the greatest nation on the face of the earth. They have such a notorious reputation that within three centuries the whole known world is talking about Israel. A queen from the Saudi Arabian peninsula hears of this great kingdom and decides she will check it out first hand. She travels north, passing the crossing to Egypt, the former greatest nation. Her journey continues further north toward Canaan. Listen to these words:

---

5. *Deuteronomy 4:5-8*

1 Kings 10:1-10

1 When the queen of Sheba heard about the fame of Solomon and his relation to the name of the LORD, she came to test him with hard questions.

2 Arriving at Jerusalem with a very great caravan – with camels carrying spices, large quantities of gold, and precious stones – she came to Solomon and talked with him about all that she had on her mind.

3 Solomon answered all her questions; nothing was too hard for the king to explain to her.

4 When the queen of Sheba saw all the wisdom of Solomon and the palace he had built,

5 the food on his table, the seating of his officials, the attending servants in their robes, his cupbearers, and the burnt offerings he made at the temple of the LORD, she was overwhelmed.

6 She said to the king, "The report I heard in my own country about your achievements and your wisdom is true.

7 But I did not believe these things until... I came and saw with my own eyes. Indeed, not even half was told me; in wisdom and wealth you have far exceeded the report I heard.

8 How happy your men must be! How happy your officials, who continually stand before you and hear your wisdom!

9 Praise be to the LORD your God, who has delighted in you and placed you on the throne of Israel. Because of the LORD's eternal love for Israel, he has made you king, to maintain justice and righteousness."

10 And she gave the king 120 talents of gold, large quantities of spices, and precious stones. Never again were so many spices brought in as those the queen of Sheba gave to King Solomon.

God Made A Promise And Fulfilled It

God had made a promise to build a great nation and He did it. He built a great nation in every category. Israel had just laws. They were economically prosperous. Their architecture and crafts were brilliant. They had superior education and wisdom. One of their kings, Solomon, was a great scientist. They were even admired by their former slave masters, the

Egyptians. They were by no means a perfect kingdom; God had never indicated that He was promising that. But, they were a great kingdom. This history of Israel is not written as an allegory from which we are to learn the benefits of salvation alone, although you could make that point from the text. This is history – it happened in time and space to real people, to a real nation. The point for us is: if God did it once, He can do it again. God's truth, if it is applied, can, and does, transform communities and nations. If God can develop these poor Jews into a great nation, He can do it for any existing nation in any age because not one community or nation in this world today is worse off than the Israelites in that wilderness.

God has told us to reach every creature with the message of salvation, and He has taught us how to do that. He left us the model of Jesus and Paul and the New Testament church to guide us into the global vision of reaching every language, every tribe, and every people. But God has also told us to "disciple every nation." How do we do that? God has not given us a job and then been silent on how to accomplish it. Just as the keys to evangelism are in the story and life of Jesus and Paul, the keys to our job in transforming communities are in the story and life of Moses. Israel – its journey from slavery to greatness – is our Old Testament template of how to disciple a nation!

Now the question is, "Will we learn how to use it?" Will we take the time to study God's Word until our minds have been restored, until we understand God's principles of community and nation-building in every arena of life? Will we do the work of being reformed in our generation so that God can once again glorify Himself through the wisdom and influence of His people? We must decide. You must decide.

CHAPTER 5
Learning To Color... Again!

"Then all the people went away to eat and drink, to send portions of food and to celebrate with great joy, because they now understood the words that had been made known to them."

Nehemiah 8:12

"He sent forth his word and healed them; he rescued them from the grave."

Psalm 107:20

As the woman boarded the plane and walked through my section, she peered into my open briefcase and asked, "Will we be coloring on the flight today?" There in my bag beside my Bible lay eight colored pencils. As soon as I realized what God was saying to me in the grain field revelation, I knew what I must do. At first chance I must buy colored pencils and a new Bible to study what God's Word teaches about each area of influence in society – government, economics, family, and so forth. I would start with the books of Moses because it was obviously his job to teach a nation these things. Then I would work my way through the rest of the Bible to see the whole counsel of God's Word on any given domain. I don't think I had been this excited about something since the invention of television.

I already had an idea of the domains I would study in scripture because the University of the Nations, where I was Founding International Dean of the College of Communication, had been developed around the concept that certain spheres of influence disciple nations. I chose government, economics, family, science (including technology), arts and entertainment, communication, education and, of course, the traditional work of the church. My thought, as I began, was that the very study itself would confirm whether or not these were primary categories in God's Word. The nature of the search was to discover how much each category was emphasized and what principles were given. At this same time, I came across a Bible color-coded by the traditional salvation and witnessing themes. It's a wonderful tool for studying what the Bible has to say about those subjects and I was encouraged that I was on the right track in using different colors for studying each domain. I started coloring.

The Bible Study Headache

From day one, this study was so intense that I could do only twenty or thirty minutes at a time. It required such a radical shift from how I'd been trained to read the Word that it gave me a headache. I felt my eyes were literally being distorted in their sockets. I was so profoundly affected in the reading that I would have to get up, pace the room, and pray for help to absorb all that God was saying, all that I had missed in nearly thirty years of Bible study. My secular/sacred, dichotomized mind kept rising up in rebellion against what I saw in the Word and it accused me of socializing the gospel and secularizing the Word of God. However, as I prayed and studied and sought God's help, I saw that God was teaching about all of life. God was teaching government. If this was secular, then God was secular. It was not my place to tell God in what arenas He could involve Himself. It was, rather, God's place to tell me of what His Kingdom was comprised. Day after day for five years, my mind was blown by the lost gospel of the Kingdom. I saw, time and again, where great men and women of God found the principles they had used to change and disciple their nations – principles and values that were clear in scripture, values to which we still gave lip service in so-called Christian nations, principles we no longer taught, no longer understood, and could no longer articulate with the authority of scripture behind them.

I grieved to see how much of the Word of God we no longer use because it does not fit what we emphasize and teach. I realized how much scripture we distort beyond recognition in order to teach our own interests. All of this process was deeply personal as I had spent a lifetime studying and teaching these very distortions. I had traveled to nearly half the world's nations giving them less than twenty percent of God's counsel. I had led discipleship programs for more than half of my life that never touched on eighty percent of the nature and character of God and His perfect ways in all of life.

I Will Die Of Splendor

On the other hand, while I grieved that I had only seen a small portion of God's revelation of Himself, I equally rejoiced and worshiped the God I had never known being revealed to me. I wanted to run from my study and shout from the rooftops, "You have no idea how great God is! You have no idea how great God's good news is!" My heart literally raced with the revelation of the completeness and unsurpassable greatness of the lordship of Christ and His kingdom. Salvation, and the life that it gave me, was the turning point in my life, but it was nothing compared to the daily revelation of the rest of the gospel and the greatness of His kingdom. As I had thought I would die of need so many years ago in Hawaii, I now felt I would die from the splendor of God's revelation of Himself.

In reducing the gospel to salvation alone, we had also reduced our revelation of God to Savior. Indeed, He is our Savior. This is a wonderful revelation and it is a revelation essential to entering the gates of His kingdom. However, we have lost the revelation of: the King of Kings, the Lord of justice...Jehovah Jireh, Lord of economics...the Father, Lord of the family...the Creator God, Lord of science and technology...the Living Word, Lord of communication...the Potter, Lord of the arts and beauty...the Great Teacher, Lord of education. We use these names and we worship these images, but we no longer understand the supremacy of Christ in each of these domains and vocations.

We Have A "Miniature" Jesus

Today, we reflect a "miniature" Jesus, by getting saved and then standing inside the door of the Kingdom, calling others to salvation. We do not know how to move past the cloakroom into the greatness of God in all of life. We don't know how to think about God's political agenda. We don't know what the gospel has to say about building our lives and communities economically. We don't know how to keep our marriages together. We don't have time for secular activities like the arts. We huddle in the foyer of God's great mansion and try to define ourselves there because our lives have less and less to do with the outside world. Is it any wonder, then, that we fixate on experiences and feelings, seeking refuge from the world we live in rather than engaging it? If our minds are not challenged and we are closed off from all of life except getting saved, what is left?

For nearly a decade at this writing, I have been looking at the scriptures from the perspective of God's teaching on the domains. I have colored my entire Bible many times: what God says about government, education, economics, family, the arts, communication, science, and the church. Daily, my mind, my spirit, and my heart explode with gratitude for who God is and the treasures He has given us in Christ Jesus. I am not ashamed of this gospel because it is relevant to all man's needs and all the issues we face today.

In Part II, I hope to give you the beginnings of this great revelation of the nature and character of God revealed in all that He has made. These ideas just scratch the surface of the Word. This is a lifetime study, and I am calling you to join me on the journey, the journey back to the gospel of the kingdom – the journey back to the God of all things.

Are you hungry? Join me in the feast!

PART II

OLD TESTAMENT
TEMPLATE

How Do We Get Started?

In Part II we begin to look at what the Bible teaches us about the various domains of society and the principles that are to guide us in our involvement in these arenas. It is important to remember that this first volume of the "Old Testament Template" is an introduction to the concepts and ideas. It is in no way exhaustive of what the Bible has to say about each domain. In future works we hope to look at each domain more completely from all of scripture. But that study and research is still in process and will come later. Here we are trying to learn how to study and rethink what scripture has to say about these areas. In reordering our thinking to match the mind of Christ it is important for us to rethink carefully and methodically, laying down percept after precept, digesting them, incorporating them into our lives in obedience to truth and His Lordship, and *then* ask the Holy Spirit to lead us to the next level of understanding. I am trying to follow this radical obedience in my own life and mind, resisting the temptation to run off with a lot of easy and premature conclusions. People ask me every time I teach to draw conclusions and applications to current events that I am simply not prepared to make yet. God is renewing my mind. God is taking my thinking captive. It is a process and the most destructive thing we can do is to get ahead of Him, thinking we know more of what the Word of God says than we actually do. Lord, help us in our temptations.

In this section we will look at examples of what the Bible, primarily Deuteronomy, teaches us about each domain and how to track those principles through the rest of scripture. There are many principles on many different levels in every domain. We will only look at a few. The primary point is to begin changing how we read and think about scripture in ways that move us toward an integrated view of God and all of life. We have used Deuteronomy as the basis of most of the introduction because the Jewish scholars accepted it as the foundation book of what Moses was teaching in all his writings. All future scholarship, including that of Jesus and Paul, will reference back to Moses and the teachings imparted by God through him as the foundation stones of biblical thinking.

Each domain reveals attributes of God's character and nature. Each domain reveals truths about His Kingdom and how it functions. When we study these areas we are studying about God. Not only what He does but who He is! It is essential that we keep this our focus and our passion. If we study with strategy and action as our primary motive we will miss the heart of the message. God's primary objective is not to get us to fulfill a job for Him, even one as important as reaching and discipling the nations. God's primary desire for you and me is to reveal Himself to us. He wants us to know Him! This humbles my heart. This humbles my mind. What kind of God is this that cares so much for you and me that He desires to know and to be known with such intimacy? This truth of God's priorities must supersede all other motives in our search for a relevant gospel to the issues of the 21st Century.

It is not, first and foremost, about us and what we are to do. It is about Him!

CHAPTER 6
Government

"And the government will be on His shoulders."

Isaiah 9:6

"This is also why you pay taxes, for the authorities are God's servants, who give their full time to governing."

Romans 13:6

For more than a generation many, if not most, Christians have thought of the domain of government as the bastion of cigar-smoking egomaniacs. I have heard prominent men of God say that they see no way a Christian could be involved in politics without compromising their faith in Christ. This thinking is so extreme in parts of the body of Christ that some churches teach their members not to vote because it is a "secular" activity. This is a profound example of the split thinking of secular vs. sacred.

When the blacks in Namibia were first given the vote they elected a communist government, a heavy blow in a country where more than eighty-five percent of the population are professing Christians.[1] But there was a ray of hope when the newly seated government sent word to church leaders in the nation that they wished representatives of the church to come and teach them the biblical basis of government. What a privilege! However, no one responded! In South Africa the ruling party today (with sixty-five percent of the vote, reported to be around seventy percent Christian) struggles to stay in power, in part, they say, because the theology of some churches has produced a non-participatory culture among Christians when it comes to social, political and economic issues. I am told by American government officials

---

1. *Patrick Johnstone, "Operation World", 1986*

that far less than fifty percent of American citizens vote. But more shocking, they say that less than twenty-five percent of American Christians vote.

All of this is a far cry from the respect Paul accorded those who sought to serve in the government arena.[2] Jesus understood that government had a role in His Father's Kingdom. He was discipled *by* the Old Testament, and He discipled *with* the Old Testament. Jesus understood that He was the King of Kings and that His message was a message of salvation and a message of political justice.

The King Of Kings

When we study the domain of government in the Bible, we are looking at areas like the legislative, executive, judicial, and military functions of government. We are looking at law, national and local authority, relationships between nations, rules of war, and areas of community development related to government. We are looking at the roles and actions of judges and kings and those who worked for them in official capacities. Books like Joshua, Judges, I & II Samuel, I & II Kings, and I & II Chronicles unfold events happening in and to Israel in the political arena. They document what the political leaders of Israel were doing, how they affected Israel, and what God thought about these events. Nehemiah, Esther, and Daniel tell us the stories of people who sought to serve God faithfully in the political arena. Interestingly, Nehemiah, Esther, and Daniel each served pagan and idolatrous nations and kingdoms. Today, some Christians believe we can serve only the righteous in government. But scripture does not bear this out. Psalms, Proverbs, Ecclesiastes, and Song of Solomon were written primarily, and possibly in their entirety, by two kings, David and Solomon. Each of these books teaches us much besides the principles of government, but the position from which they were written was the realm of government, unlike Isaiah, or Jeremiah, and other books written from the perspective of prophets.

In my study of Deuteronomy, about twenty-five percent of the book is given to instructions and episodes revolving around government issues. The passage we will use for our sample study of the domain of government is Deuteronomy 1:9-18. Moses had been attempting to sit as judge

---

2. *Romans 13:6*

by himself over the disputes of the entire Israelite population. His father-in-law had suggested to him that this was not going to work and that he needed to initiate the levels of government to carry the load of arbitrating the judicial needs of the nation. In Deuteronomy, Moses forms Israel's first system of government. Here is the account:

Deuteronomy 1:9-18

9 At that time I said to you, "You are too heavy a burden for me to carry alone.

10 The LORD your God has increased your numbers so that today you are as many as the stars in the sky.

11 May the LORD, the God of your fathers, increase you a thousand times and bless you as he has promised!

12 But how can I bear your problems and your burdens and your disputes all by myself?

13 Choose some wise, understanding and respected men from each of your tribes, and I will set them over you."

14 You answered me, "What you propose to do is good."

15 So I took the leading men of your tribes, wise and respected men, appointed them to have authority over you – as commanders of thousands, of hundreds, of fifties and of tens and as tribal officials.

16 And I charged your judges at that time: Hear the disputes between your brothers and judge fairly, whether the case is between brother Israelites or between one of them and an alien.

17 Do not show partiality in judging; hear both small and great alike. Do not be afraid of any man, for judgment belongs to God. Bring me any case too hard for you, and I will hear it.

18 And at that time I told you everything you were to do.

For our purpose here of learning to read and study the Bible in order to see God's principles in each domain, we will take only the highlights of the passage. Remember that the truths of the Bible are told primarily in story form. We study the history and context, but we will never be in the same circumstances as Moses and Israel, so their application will not necessarily work for us. The principles, however, are God's truth and are applicable in new and dynamic ways in any age, any set of circumstances in any nation. Let's work with this passage as an example of extracting principles from the historical situation.

The Purpose Of Government

Deuteronomy 1:9-12
9 At that time I said to you, "You are too heavy a burden for me to carry alone.
10 The LORD your God has increased your numbers so that today you are as many as the stars in the sky.
11 May the LORD, the God of your fathers, increase you a thousand times and bless you as he has promised!
12 But how can I bear your problems and your burdens and your disputes all by myself?

As Moses prepared to form Israel's first formal government, he explained to the people the purpose of government and why Israel needed to move away from him as their sole leader. Moses had been carrying the load by himself until now. But this system no longer fulfilled the objective of government. What was that objective? Moses saw it as his responsibility to hear the burdens and disputes of the people in order to provide just resolution. Moses did not argue that the disputes were not important or that they ought not to be disputing in the first place. He did not see disputes as insignificant matters or a waste of his time. He established that they must be heard and dealt with, but Israel had grown so large in Egypt that the former tribal system of governing themselves no longer worked. They needed a more effective system. Why? To meet the judicial needs of the people!

One of the foundational principles in this passage is that the primary purpose of government is to serve the population of a nation by providing an objective, trustworthy source of arbitration and justice. The system of government was organized in such a way that it could serve the needs of people both "small and great" alike (vs.17). God looked at the judicial needs of the people and the fact that the current system was not meeting those needs. He inspired Moses in his role of creating a structure of government that would respond to the judicial needs of the nation at large and set out to put it in place.

The Authority Of Government

1:13 "Choose some wise, understanding and respected men from each of your tribes, and I will set them over you."

From the perspective of government in the Bible, I think this is one of the most thrilling verses. Think about it. This nation of people had lived in exile for 430 years. For 300 of those years they had been slaves under the total authority of the Egyptian government. Their experience of leadership prior to their years in Egypt was more that of a large family, some seventy people, rather than that of ruling a nation. We can assume that many of the Jews, if not most, were uneducated people. They had lived in poverty and there was certainly no reason for the Egyptians to expend their national budget for educating their slaves. At this time they were still in the wilderness, exiles in a "no man's land," with no tangible assets except what they carried on their backs.

Moses was God's man, a man who spoke with God face to face. God had been giving Moses detailed instructions for leading Israel to freedom. He had given Moses incredible authority by bringing to pass everything Moses had said would happen. If anyone ever had a direct line to God, it was Moses. When he formed government in Israel, how did God tell him to do it?

"Choose some wise, understanding and respected men..." Who chose the leadership? Moses? Aaron and Miriam? No, the people of Israel! The very first thing that God did through Moses when establishing government was to give the people the right and authority to choose.

What an amazing God! In all of His infinite knowledge and wisdom God did not impose His will. He could have said to Moses, "You choose some wise and understanding men and put them over Israel." That would have been more like the model they had seen in Egypt. That would have been more like what was being modeled by the tribal nations surrounding them. But God did something so radical, so dangerous, so not of this world, that we are still trying to grapple with the principle in our modern age. He gave the people of Israel the right to choose their political leaders.

We could say, then, that a second principle of government is that **God gives the authority of governance to the people.** God delegated by law and decree to the people the right and responsibility of choosing who would rule over them. He made it a bottom up authority as opposed to the top down authority of the Egyptian pharaohs. He gave the people power.

Many people today, in and out of Christian circles, believe the important thing is to tell the public what to do. We often assume that people do not have the experience, the education, the grasp of issues to make proper choices. Surely it would be better to start them off gradually and nurture them into the process of responsibility. But God began the process of discipling Israel in their new freedom by giving them the responsibility to choose who would lead them.

This principle is profoundly supported throughout the biblical history of Israel, a nation ruled by judges for some 470 years. The people observed and interacted with the nations surrounding them, and saw that these nations had kings. Israel liked this idea! Israel had some good judges, but they had some real losers topped off by the notorious Samson. They decided they needed a king, and told Samuel, the prophet to the nation.[3] Samuel sought God and God responded very clearly. He did *not* want them to have a king, and He gave them a very sizable list of reasons why. But the people persisted. They wanted a king! God relented and told Samuel they could choose what they wanted. Think about this! God gave them the king that He did not want because that is what they chose. A king was not the best choice, but this is what they, as a nation, chose. God had given the people the authority to choose their political leaders, and, having made His preference known, He stuck to that principle. Israel decided to have a king, and God sought to help them choose a king. God went beyond sticking to His principles, He sought to bless the kings that Israel chose. Saul, David, and Solomon were all mightily used by God, but they were still the system of governance He did not want.

Perhaps you are thinking, "But didn't the prophets actually choose the kings?" This is fascinating to track in scripture. God did use the prophets to point to the leader He thought would serve their best interests. At

3. *1 Samuel 8*

God's direction they anointed these leaders with oil, prayed and prophesied over them.[4] But we do not see a king in Israel actually crowned king until we hear words something like, "All Israel gathered and took so and so as their king."[5] After the people made their choice, the king realized his authority.

This principle of the authority of the people to choose their political leaders is tested in the life of David. When Saul died, the Kingdom of Israel was divided over who would lead them. The House of Judah had chosen Saul's rival, David, who had already been anointed to be king over Israel by Samuel. But Saul had a son, Ish-Bosheth, and Israel chose him to be their king. Two leaders of Ish-Bosheth's raiding bands decided David should be King of Israel as well as Judah. They murdered Ish-Bosheth and took his head to David. Rather than accept their offer to be king, David executes them for the murder.[6] He remains in Hebron until all the tribes of Israel came to David and asked him to be King.[7]

David understood, having studied the books of Moses, that God had given the authority of choosing political leaders to the people.

We have to wonder why God would design government to have its authority in the people. Wouldn't it be better for people to be told by a loving, benevolent God what is best for them? Evidently not. This subject is too broad to cover in this introductory volume. But it appears that the discipleship of a nation, as well as individuals, is tied to the cause-and-effect learning process of experiencing the blessing or cursing that comes automatically from making choices. In other words, it was more important for Israel to make their choice, even if it was not a perfect choice, and to learn from the consequences. Weighty implications, but they will have to wait for future study.

Character Does Matter

1:13 Choose some wise, understanding, and respected men....

God did not leave Israel floundering in a vacuum with their choices

---

4. *1 Samuel 10:1, 1 Samuel 16:13, 1 Kings 1:34*
5. *1 Samuel 10:24, 2 Samuel 2:4, 2 Samuel 5:1-3, 1 Kings 1:39-40*
6. *2 Samuel 4*
7. *2 Samuel 5:1-5*

of political leaders. He gave them guidelines. Some of those guidelines focused on character, knowledge, and the leader's reputation. A Nigerian friend once said to me that one of the big differences between a Westerner and an African is the standard we use to judge the importance of an individual. A Westerner, he felt, was more prone to assess a person by what he owned, what he did, or his position. An African, on the other hand, drew his assessment of an individual from what other people thought about that person. In other words, you had status in the tribe if the community gave you status, not because of some external, such as possessions or your work. The African approach is more relational and is tied to the character and observable actions of the individual within a community setting. When it comes to political leaders, God, it would appear, leans toward the African perspective. The people were made responsible to assess the character of the leaders they would grant political power over them, and then live with the consequences of their choices.

Moses gave Israel three things to look for in their leaders – wisdom, understanding, and respectability. Money and power, though not disqualified, are not mentioned as criteria. In order for these character attributes to be evaluated, the leaders had to be known by the people and the people had to determine what *wise and understanding* meant. What made an individual respectable? How was wisdom demonstrated? What did it mean to have understanding? As a community they not only had to search for an individual who embodied these qualities, they had to search for understanding about the nature of those qualities. They would enter a national debate on character, if you will. God was developing them as citizens, not just giving them government.

Representative

1:13 ...from each of your tribes...

From the time Israel left Egypt, God began to emphasize the importance of inclusion in the political and legal process. He reminded Israel that they must remember what it was like to be slaves who had no rights. He reminded them repeatedly that they were not to have one standard of justice for the Israelite and another for the alien. They were not to leave any tribe without representation in their new land and government. Political representation is a biblical principle. If the purpose of government is to truly represent the people by arbitrating their disputes and issues of justice, if the authority of government truly comes from the people, then the people have to be truly represented.

The great error of the South African government of the 20th Century was that one white tribe declared the right to rule over all other tribes. The right to vote was extended only to the white tribes. The black tribes were left without representation. If we understand these scriptures and that God could not bless a system that left a people disenfranchised from the powers that ruled over them, then it would come as no surprise that the South African government of this era could achieve no lasting stability. In principle it was doomed to fail. But understanding here will also lead to great admiration for the leadership of Nelson Mandela and his commitment not to form a government unless every black tribe and every white tribe was represented. The upholding of this principle safeguarded the nation and held civil war at bay. When we think of the Aboriginal in Australia, the Laplander in Finland, and the Native American Indian, we are seeing situations fraught with potential conflict because the principle of representation has been diluted or ignored altogether.

Consensus

1:14 You answered me, "What you propose to do is good."

The authority of the people is reinforced again. In this very short sentence Moses established that his plan had the backing of the nation. Israel agreed to be governed in this way.

Israel had not always agreed with Moses. In his first attempt to take them into the promised land, they said, in fear and unbelief, that they would not go. They staged what we would call today a military coup, and the men of fighting age refused to take on the challenge of the promised land in spite of Moses', Joshua's, and Caleb's exhortations.[8] God was ready for

---

8. *Numbers 14:6-9*

them to move into the promised land. Moses was ready for them to move. The people were not in agreement. The government lacked consensus and could not move ahead. Israel suffered the consequences of their choices by spending forty years in the wilderness. In the account of David's appointment as king over Israel, the house of Judah and the house of Saul did not have consensus; David waited rather than contest the will of the people.[9]

This principle of consensus is so important that Jesus refers to it as a principle of God's kingdom in the New Testament. "Every kingdom divided against itself will be ruined..."[10] **The principle is this: a nation with consensus has a more stable government.** A nation without consensus is a weakened nation. Therefore a government that tries to impose its will on the people will be less stable in the long term than a government that rules with consensus. Certainly the specific issues are also important, but that is not our subject here. However, consensus itself is clearly an important principle of government in scripture and is one of the foundations of strong government. This gives us understanding when we look at nations in crisis or certain national issues. Ireland and South Africa have been on the front pages of world news for a very long time, with both nations being in great turmoil. In *How The Irish Saved Civilization,* Thomas Cahill reveals that the Irish have never been able to agree on who governed them. For the 8,000 plus years of Irish history, their kings and tribes have been at war. Failure of a few attempts to rule themselves with an Irish king led them to seek French, Scottish, and, finally, English monarchs to rule over them. The failure to find any semblance of consensus has led to millennia of Irish turmoil. Conversely, it makes the importance of the Irish accord signed in the 1990's even more resounding. For perhaps the first time in their very long history, the Irish are beginning to see that agreement and consensus are essential if a nation is to rule itself. God is discipling Ireland.

When we look at situations today such as East Timor, former Yugoslavia, and the former Soviet Union we are seeing, in part, the fruit of rule forced on a people with little or no involvement, let alone any level of consensus.

---

9. *2 Samuel 5:1*
10. *Matthew 12:25*

The Judicial Branch

Deuteronomy 1:16-18

16 And I charged your judges at that time: Hear the disputes between your brothers and judge fairly, whether the case is between brother Israelites or between one of them and an alien.

17 Do not show partiality in judging; hear both small and great alike. Do not be afraid of any man, for judgment belongs to God. Bring me any case too hard for you, and I will hear it.

18 And at that time I told you everything you were to do.

Now Moses turned his attention to the judicial purpose of government and began to give instructions to those who would hear the disputes of the people. These verses lay down such powerful principles of justice that every just court in the world uses them, and every court on earth today would be more just if the principles were thoroughly implemented. First, verse 16 exhorts Israel's judges to judge fairly. Moses goes on to define *fairly* very specifically. *Fairly* means extending the same quality of justice to every individual whether they were Israelite or alien, national or foreigner. This is a major theme in God's discipleship of Israel. Over and over again in their biblical history God reminds them of what it was like to be slaves under the authority of Egypt, what it was like to be a foreigner and unjustly treated, and what it was like to be disenfranchised from the justice system of the nation they were in. He used this tragic part of their history to call them to a higher level of justice in their own nation. Justice in Israel was to be blind to nationality, color, gender, creed, or politics. Justice was to have a level playing field and to treat all people equally.

In verse 17, Israel's judicial system was exhorted to **judge without partiality** and a second class distinction is given: their court system was not to draw a distinction between "small and great." Justice in Israel was not to be tilted toward the powerful and influential or the rich. All people were to be heard. The slave in Egypt had no voice and God told Israel that they were to demonstrate a higher level of justice in their nation.

Moses reminded them that justice belongs to God. As judges, they were not to be afraid of other people, powers, or influences. **They were to remember that, as governmental agents of justice, they stood first and foremost before God.** God understood that the human race was fallen and prone to sin and that the Jews, being human, would be just as prone to corruption as any other group of people or any nation. He was challenging them to rise above this in their system of government. Moses laid down the last principle of the judicial system in this passage. **There is to be a process of appeal.** For cases too hard for a finding, or when findings and evidence were inconclusive, the system allowed another hearing – this time before Moses.

Some years ago I was privileged to speak at a conference where a head of state sat directly before me in the front row. This man was a Christian political leader in a pagan nation. His desire was to use his office to influence his nation for righteousness. When I inquired about the judicial system in his country, I found that the president hires and fires at will all judges in this nation. It is good that the president is concerned for the souls of his people, and I mean that with all sincerity. But the president could move his nation toward God by changing the justice system as well. In this country, a judge faced with a less than obvious finding, knowing he could lose his livelihood, might favor the preference of the president who holds his job in his hand. This is human nature. And God never forgets that man is fallen. He lays down every principle and system with our fallen state in mind. One judge can be corrupted some of the time, but it is harder to corrupt two judges in an appeal, and so forth. God understands that without checks and balances in the system, fallen people will abuse power and corrupt justice.

Summary

We looked at five basic principles of government from nine verses in Deuteronomy.
1. Government is ordained by God and essential to the life of a nation.
2. Government gets its authority from the people.
3. The character of a political leader is important and to be weighed by the people in their choices.

4. Government is to be representative of all people.

5. One of government's primary purposes is to provide a source of just resolution to disputes and conflicts of the people.

The primary purpose of this introductory volume is not to teach a complete biblical approach to government or any other domain. Our purpose is to reveal how our split Christian thinking has alienated us from God's great wisdom and teaching in each domain and to demonstrate how God's Word teaches us principles for all of life, as we have seen in these verses on government. In order to get the mind of Christ on government, we are going to have to study the subject from Genesis to Revelation and get the whole counsel of God on the subject. This will take time and patience. It took Moses forty years to lay down God's teaching in the wilderness. We need a generation of faithful Bible students to help us reinherit the truth. Are you one of them? Start now!

One great reformer said that peace is not just the absence of conflict: it is the presence of justice. When we pray for peace, let us remember God requires that we be involved in working for justice.

STUDY HELP:

Themes to look for in studying and coloring government in the scriptures are: *law; government; the military; legislative, executive, and judicial branches of government; national and local authority; and community development from the legislative or executive perspective.*

The domain of government reveals: **The King of Kings**

The primary attribute of God revealed in government: **Justice**

God governs this domain through: **Delegation of authority to the people**

The color I used: **Purple**

WORKING VOCATIONAL MISSION STATEMENT:

To provide and ensure justice and equity for all citizens including executive, judicial, military, law enforcement and central community services. **Great issues include:** justice for the weak and voiceless in society including children, women, and immigrants.

NOTE TO ALL BELIEVERS:

God is calling you to be a good citizen as part of the witness of your faith. Political action and interest are not "secular" in the sense that they are not important for the believer. God instituted government, and He gave you and me responsibility for it. God is just and wants all His people to work for justice. First of all, it is our responsibility under God to be informed and to be involved. Do you vote? If you live in a country where participation is allowed, it is your moral obligation as a Christian to be involved. If you live in a country where you are denied that right, you must pray and work to see your nation's legal system changed. As believers we should be volunteering at the polls, helping people get registered, and making it possible to have a place to vote. We should explain to our children that God gave us this great right and responsibility to be involved in our political life, and we must cherish and safeguard this right. As believers we are to believe that our involvement makes a difference because it makes a difference to God. We are to teach our children that serving in government is a high calling, and if God has gifted our children in this area then He may call them and favor them as He did David, Daniel, Joseph, Nehemiah, and others. If this is the case, they will have a much higher purpose in their occupations than "just making money." They must know that they serve God and must have the mind of Christ, the power of the Holy Spirit, and strategic prayer support if their work is to accomplish something of lasting value for the Kingdom.

You are God's strategy for discipling your community and nation. Will you respond to the call?

A NOTE TO THE GOVERNMENT PROFESSIONAL:

If you are a lawyer, judge, police officer, civil servant, soldier, elected official, social worker, or serve your nation's government in any capacity, you have a high calling from God. The pillars of God's kingdom are justice and righteousness, and your calling is to support the pillar of justice. You are challenged by scripture to be God's extension of His justice to the people whom you serve. It does not matter if you work in a system that is fair as Solomon did, or in one that is somewhat or thoroughly unjust as Joseph and Daniel did; you have a calling from God to give and work for the highest level of justice possible in the system. First, you must be just in your own dealings with people; then you must work to make the institutions, systems, and laws just. What would your nation look like if every Christian professional made this their passion and pursued it with a sense of call? God will start with one. Are you that one? Will you study to take on the mind of Christ in the political arena and apply what you are learning first to your own life and work, and then, where possible, to the institutions themselves? You are God's strategy for discipling your nation.

CHAPTER 7
Economics

"However, there should be no poor among you, for in the land the Lord your God is giving you to possess as your inheritance, he will richly bless you."

Deuteronomy 15:4

"For the kingdom of heaven is like a landowner who went out early in the morning to hire men to work in his vineyard."

Matthew 20:1

"Money is the root of all evil!" "Filthy lucre!" Common enough ideas in the mind of many Christians today. "If you love God you will despise material gain" is a prevalent undercurrent in Christianity. "If I truly love God, I will probably be poor" is, perhaps, not taught, but it is surely thought. The split thinking that creates a false divide between the spiritual and material is as glaringly obvious in this domain as any other. God's promises to Israel as they left slavery in Egypt were not confined to blessings of an unseen nature. He promised He would bless them in every area of life including their crops, livestock, and business. He encouraged that if they would obey His teachings, they would not have poverty in their land. God fulfilled His promise. In little more than 300 years, Israel moved from having abject poverty in the wilderness to being one of the wealthiest nations in its day.

For most of the first two millennia of church growth, economic change and development followed the spread of the gospel. In Norway, Hans Nielsen Hauge, an early evangelist, worked his way from one desperately poor village to another. As he planted churches he also taught biblical business practices and helped new converts start businesses. Not only were souls won in Scandinavia and the rest of western Europe, but the gospel fed an economic revolution. Moses taught that Israel was to have no poor and the early church began to deal with poverty in its earliest agendas. Moses taught that work was part of our service to God and Paul reaffirmed this in the New Testament by teaching that believers who did not work did not eat.[1]

This is a far cry from the fruit the gospel has produced over the last two centuries. Africa probably provides us with our most stark reality. In his book, *Hope For Africa – And What The Christian Can Do,* Dr. George Kinoti, a university professor in Kenya, lays out the following crucial observations: One out of every three Africans does not get enough to eat. By 1987, 55 to 60 percent of rural Africans were living below the poverty line and the rate of impoverishment is accelerating. Two thirds of the poorest 40 nations in the world are African, as are eight of the poorest ten nations. "Experts tell us that Christianity is growing faster in Africa than on any other continent. At the same time, the people are rapidly becoming poorer and the moral and social fabric of society are disintegrating fast. Christianity is clearly not making a significant difference to African nations."[2]

It is not uncommon today to find believers who think of money more in terms of magic than in terms of biblical principles. *"If I give this amount, I will get this amount back! God will drop provision from the sky. I am believing for a miracle in my finances."*

Please! Understand me here. I am not against tithing. I believe God can and does perform financial miracles, and I believe God honors and blesses the generous heart. However, this thinking, when separated from scripture's overarching principles of finance, is not "biblical" thinking, it is mysticism. Let's look at a key economic passage from Moses' teaching in Deuteronomy:

Deuteronomy 15:1-10
1 At the end of every seven years you must cancel debts.
2 This is how it is to be done: Every creditor shall cancel the loan he has made to his fellow Israelite. He shall not require payment from his fellow Israelite or brother, because the LORD's time for canceling debts has been proclaimed.

---

1. *2 Thessalonians 3:10*
2. *"Hope for Africa" Ibid. page 12*

3 You may require payment from a foreigner, but you must cancel any debt your brother owes you.
4 However, there should be no poor among you, for in the land the LORD your God is giving you to possess as your inheritance, he will richly bless you,
5 if only you fully obey the LORD your God and are careful to follow all these commands I am giving you today.
6 For the LORD your God will bless you as he has promised, and you will lend to many nations but will borrow from none. You will rule over many nations but none will rule over you.
7 If there is a poor man among your brothers in any of the towns of the land that the LORD your God is giving you, do not be hard-hearted or tight-fisted towards your poor brother.
8 Rather be open-handed and freely lend him whatever he needs.
9 Be careful not to harbor this wicked thought: "The seventh year, the year for canceling debts, is near," so that you do not show ill will towards your needy brother and give him nothing. He may then appeal to the LORD against you, and you will be found guilty of sin.
10 Give generously to him and do so without a grudging heart; then because of this the LORD your God will bless you in all your work and in everything you put your hand to.

God makes it clear throughout scripture that it is His desire to bless *all* nations.[3] When we ask, "How does God want to bless them?", we find the answer in how He blessed Israel. Economic blessing was a clear part of God's design for Israel from the moment they left Egypt. In Deuteronomy 15 we see that while they are still in the wilderness, He is beginning to prepare them for economic development and their responsibility for both the individual and the nation.

Debt Is To Be Limited

15:1 At the end of every seven years you must cancel debts.
2 This is how it is to be done: Every creditor shall cancel the loan he has made to his fellow Israelite. He shall not require payment from his

---

3. *Genesis 12:3; 18:18; 22:18; 26:4; 28:14*

fellow Israelite or brother, because the LORD's time for canceling debts has been proclaimed.
3 You may require payment from a foreigner, but you must cancel any debt your brother owes you.

When I speak in various countries I often ask how many in my audience have heard the teaching that Christians should never borrow. No matter what region of the world I am in, a few have been exposed to this message. The text that is often used for this teaching is, "Let no debt remain outstanding."[4] Basic rules of Bible study, however, tell us we must interpret scripture with scripture. We cannot make any single text mean something that makes nonsense out of other scriptural injunctions since there are many scriptures giving instructions for how to lend, how to borrow, and guidelines for repayment. Romans 13:8 does not literally mean "do not borrow." It means do not default on your loan, make your payments on time, and keep your contracted agreement.

Here in verses one through three Moses is giving instruction for a system of debt repayment in Israel. It is unlikely that any nation is going to use the application of a seven-year national cycle again; but remember our task is to extract the principle from the purpose this application would accomplish. **The principle here is that debt is to be limited.** Israelites were not allowed to encumber people with debt in perpetuity. The system in Israel was universal. All of Israel's private debt was forgiven in the same year. If you borrowed in the first year of the cycle you had seven years to repay. If you borrowed in the third year you had four years to repay and so forth. When the lender and the borrower entered into an agreement, they had to come up with a repayment plan that fit within the time.

My own country, the United States, has some of the best and worst examples of obeying this principle. When it comes to buying homes, America has a wonderful system. The interest rate is required by law to be one of the lowest rates for any loan, and the mortgage repayment plan must be for fifteen or thirty years. This system has made the United States one of the largest private home-owning populations in the world. On the other hand, America's credit card system is more or less out of control. When you graduate from college, and often now even from high school, you get

---

4. *Romans 13:8*

two, three or even more unsolicited credit cards in the mail. Each card gives you instant access to $1000 to $5000 dollars of credit. Many young people and many not so young people use these cards without ever looking at the fine print where it says the interest rate may be 19 to 26 percent or higher. I have seen interest rates as high as 36 percent. If you follow the seductive plan and pay only the "small minimum payment" required you will pay back the original amount thirty or forty times. You begin to pay interest upon interest. At one time this would have been called "loan-sharking" and would have been illegal. Today it is the norm for credit card payments in many countries. America's personal credit card debt is greater than the national debt and undermines the stability of the nation's economy.

It would seem from the broad look at finances in the first five books of the Bible, that loaning was essential to enabling people to get out of their poverty. The lending focus was on small business loans. The purpose of these loans was to get people out of need and able to provide for themselves. The goal was economic enablement. For generations Jews have continued to practice many of these principles, the result being that no matter where you go in the world, no matter how poor the country, if Jews are there, they are making money. That does not mean that there are never poor Jews or that all Jews are wealthy, but they get established quickly and provide for themselves. Having an understanding of the purpose of lending, one Jewish family migrates and gets established. They send for the next family and loan them money to get started. That money is either repaid or is then loaned for the next family to come and get established. Lending, as Moses taught it, was about helping people get on their feet financially and becoming a productive part of the community. Lending was primarily a part of community responsibility and, secondly, a way of making money.

I have been told about a Christian banker who, studying these scriptures, was challenged that in America the banking system is loaning to the wrong people or perhaps it is better to say it is not loaning to the right people. U.S.A. banking institutions tend to loan to the wealthy or those who already have debt. But these same institutions will rarely accept a loan for the immigrant, women, the unemployed, or the poor who have a plan for starting a business but have no capital, but also no debt. This man began a private bank that only loaned to people who had a good idea for becoming a productive part of the community and only needed the money to get started. The bank has been enormously successful and has never had a defaulted loan. This is biblical economics.

Let's take another look at verse three. "You may require payment from a foreigner, but you must cancel any debt your brother owes you." At first glance one could think that God does not care about foreigners as much as He cares about Israel. This is not true. Again, the apparent meaning here cannot be the accurate meaning because it makes nonsense out of many other scriptures. It is clear from Genesis to Revelation that God wants to bless all nations. This theme is so overwhelming that it cannot be contested. Then why didn't God require debt forgiveness for foreigners? The most probable interpretation of this variance is that the Jews were required to take the eighth year as a sabbatical year. They could not work nor could they work their animals or land. Therefore, they could not make payments. The non-Jews however were not required to obey this Jewish law. They could continue to work and they could make payments. In fact this was probably a "wind fall" year for the non-Jewish immigrants helping to enable them economically.

No Poor Among You

15:4 However, there should be no poor among you, for in the land the LORD your God is giving you to possess as your inheritance, he will richly bless you,
5 if only you fully obey the LORD your God and are careful to follow all these commands I am giving you today.

Verse four lays out a second principle we can glean from this passage. **Israel was to have a national commitment to the elimination of poverty.** Financial blessing came with financial responsibility within the nation. No teachings in scripture give a limit to personal or national wealth. There is teaching that wealth should not be your life obsession, that you should not put your trust in wealth, that wealth can draw your heart away from equally important things if you are not careful. However, scripture also applauds financial initiative and the role of wealth in the blessing of the community. The Bible emphasizes that the economic system of the community is to be one that is constantly addressing the elimination of poverty. For anyone to be poor and destitute in Israel was a shame on the whole community.

As I write this book, America is experiencing one of the greatest financial booms in its history. Millionaires and billionaires are being created at a monumental rate. However the test of financial stability for a nation is not only the wealth being generated, but also activity at the bottom of the economic scale. Are the poor increasing or decreasing? The U.S.A. has more billionaires and, at the same time, an increasing number of people who live under the poverty line. The problem is not wealth, per se; the problem is irresponsible making of wealth. The economics of the Bible is not communist in promoting that all must be divided up equally. However, neither does it approve the flagrant disregard of the poor and the disenfranchised. Apparently, scripture promotes the idea that a growing and stable economic environment will be fostered, in part, by the enabling of those on the bottom of the economic ladder to move up, making their contribution to the quality of life in the nation.

It seems that scripture emphasizes the responsibility of the business community in relationship to the poor more than in any other domain. Farmers were to set aside the edges of their fields so that the poor could work the gleanings. Managers were encouraged to make work for the less fortunate in the community. Government is rarely mentioned in relationship to its responsibility to the poor. The church is given responsibility for the destitute. This very important distinction needs to be looked at here.

Aid Vs. Development

For centuries, Christians and humanitarians alike have promoted the obligation of nations that have to help nations that have not. Not a bad idea, in the main, and one that has a great deal of biblical support. Much of the application of this idea, at the local community level or the national level, takes the form of aid, vis-à-vis give-away programs, the idea being that if those who have will just give some of what they have to those who have not the poverty problem will be solved. On the surface this appears logical. In practice it is devastating and counter-productive. It actually produces poverty. The basic thinking is not biblical.

For the poor, the Bible emphasizes opportunity versus aid. Aid is reserved for those who have absolutely no way of providing for themselves and will die without assistance. Israel is certainly in this kind of circumstance in the wilderness – and God provides for the Israelites. However, it's interesting that the day they stepped into the promised land the aid stopped. The day they had the feasibility to provide for themselves, God withdrew the manna. They had no more money the day the manna stopped than they did the day before, but now they had opportunity to provide for themselves. God did not want to create a dependent people, but a people who drew on the gifts, talents, and resources He had given to see them provide for themselves. **Enablement is a major theme in biblical economics.**

In everything that God does with Israel, He is working not only on their external circumstances, but also on their internal view of themselves and of God. He wants them to become self-reliant, not dependent. He wants them to see what they are able to do, to create, and to build. He is working to develop their economy, as well as their self-image and their character. The essence of discipleship is developing the inner man and, whether He is developing government or economics, God is working on the development of people, how they view themselves, and how they think.

This leads us to the next principle.

No National Debt

15:6 For the LORD your God will bless you as he has promised, and you will lend to many nations but will borrow from none. You will rule over many nations but none will rule over you.

Israel was told not to borrow. **As a nation they were to have a policy of no national debt!** In order to understand God's reasoning here, we have to ask what a no-borrowing policy would produce in a community.

First, they would have to learn to live within their means. Their wants would have to be balanced with their needs. Secondly, they would have to look into themselves as a people and learn what they were capable of doing, making, and discovering. In other words, they would be pushed towards self-reliance and away from dependence as a community.

In 20th Century India, Indira Gandhi fostered a national program called "Buy India." The basic idea was to put a moratorium on imports forcing India as a nation to learn to produce the things that they wanted. If India wanted cars, washing machines, video cassette recorders, televisions, and the like, then India was going to have to learn to produce them. The first cars, VCRs, etc. did not work very well. But, they continued to improve. India slowly decreased the build up of trade imbalance, increased employment, and developed a great sense of national pride in their ability to produce and provide for themselves. They moved farther away from dependence towards self-reliance. God gifted all peoples and nations, and part of His objective in discipleship is to see those gifts shine.

Wicked Economics

15:7 If there is a poor man among your brothers in any of the towns of the land that the LORD your God is giving you, do not be hard-hearted or tight-fisted towards your poor brother.
8 Rather be open-handed and freely lend him whatever he needs.
9 Be careful not to harbor this wicked thought: "The seventh year, the year for canceling debts, is near," so that you do not show ill will towards your needy brother and give him nothing. He may then appeal to the LORD against you, and you will be found guilty of sin.
10 Give generously to him and do so without a grudging heart; then because of this the LORD your God will bless you in all your work and in everything you put your hand to.

Again we see that God remembers that man is fallen and will not necessarily do what is right, not even His beloved Jews. Remember, when this was written they were still in the wilderness having just spent 300 years as slaves. God knows the human heart and He warned them that if He was going to bless them financially, they had to think about more than themselves. He wanted to bless them, but that blessing comes with a responsibility to the greater good of the community.

Notice in verse eight the operative word *needs*. Some Christians today think we have an obligation to give whatever anyone asks. This is not a biblical mind-set. In fact, it works against biblical principles because it can produce laziness and dependence. Notice also the important word *lend*. Lending is not the same as giving a handout. This is help to get started or offset a crisis. It implies a relationship of accountability, enough involvement in the lendee's life to assess the need, and the ability to pay back.

A Few Practical Examples

A Swiss friend told me a wonderful story of community responsibility right from the pages of reformation, past and present. Her father was a vineyard keeper, as were most in their tiny village. The village had one collectively-owned vineyard. When a villager fell on bad times, he would be given this vineyard for one or two years until he could get back on his feet. The family in need worked the vineyard and kept the produce from that season. When they had reestablished themselves, the community would pass the vineyard on to the next needy family. Generosity and community responsibility – it is all there in biblical economics.

While teaching in a missions school in Denmark, a Danish worker told of what she and other Danish missionaries had done with the Tibetan tribe with which they work. This particular nomadic tribe had lost high numbers of yaks due to several extremely harsh winters. Because the yak is the centerpiece of their survival, the tribe was in danger of starvation. The Danish missionaries knew that they would be able to raise money in the West to help the tribe and did so. They bought yaks and gave them to the most desperate families. The eager worker's question to me was, "How did we do in applying biblical economics?" My response was that they had half a revelation. And half a revelation is better than no revelation at all!

The team had seen that bringing the salvation message alone was not enough. They had to be involved in other areas of the Tibetan tribe's desperate needs. They saw a financial need and sought to address it. The problem was with their solution. I asked the worker, "What would happen to the tribe if they had another series of harsh winters?" She responded that they would be in trouble again. Exactly! The solution had not solved the problem. In fact, the solution had made the tribe more dependent because, now, when they were in similar trouble they would go to Danish missionaries for help. She responded in class with an outburst of, "Help! What can we do?" Part of the problem is the *we* in the sentence. God, in His great heart to see a people developed, wants more emphasis on *them*. First of all, the tribe needed to be involved in the decision-making. The goal of biblical economics is to move towards independence and self-reliance. With blessing, God always gives responsibility and it must be one of the goals of the solution. The tribe might decide to take the yaks and after they have two calves, give one yak back – simple loan repayment allowing the missionaries to then loan the yak to another needy family. The tribe may have wanted to set up its own system whereby it took responsibility and agreed to pass a second yak calf on to the family in greatest need. This increases self-reliance and responsibility for the blessing. It also begins the multiplication process of the original gift. The tribe may decide to take the new yaks, sell every other newborn, and set up a "disaster relief fund" for future bad winters. Now self-reliance, responsibility, and long range planning are being built into the tribe's thinking. This is biblical economic discipleship!

A Swedish friend told me another wonderful story. While on business in a major African city, this businessman was awakened in the middle of the night. He could not get back to sleep and felt that God was urging him to go for a walk. As soon as he stepped out onto the street, little boys selling candy surrounded him. They slept on the street in hope of a chance night sale. These children were destitute; every penny counted. The businessman struck up a conversation with the boys and with one in particular named David. He asked them how they lived and unraveled a tale of poverty, near starvation, homelessness, and slavery by any other name. The boys' owner gave them candy and sent them out into the street to sell it. They received 15 percent of their sales. This income barely kept them from starving.

My friend found that the value of their box of candy was approximately fifteen American dollars. He told the boys that he was a Christian and a follower of Jesus and that Jesus cared about their condition and wanted to help them. He asked David whether he could live better if he sold his own candy and could keep the profits. The boy responded that he would have more than enough. My Swedish friend made a proposal to the boy: he would give him fifteen dollars to buy his own candy. When David started making extra money he agreed to save. When he had fifty dollars he would help the next boy buy his own candy and that boy would then do the same and so forth. The eager positive response was clear. He gave David the fifteen dollars and left.

Some months later a letter arrived in Sweden with the news from David that all the boys now owned their own candy. All the boys my Swedish friend had met that night had enough to eat and places to stay. All the boys were now Christians, going to church and were now helping other children get off the street. This is biblical economics: generosity, self-reliance, independence, responsibility, and multiplication all in one.

Summary

We are just skimming the surface of what the Bible has to say on these subjects. Remember, the purpose of this volume is to get us started thinking and studying the Bible in new ways. We will have to do a great deal of homework before we are ready to articulate a biblical view of economics from the whole of scripture.

The economic principles in Deuteronomy 15:1-10 we looked at:

1. Limit personal debt.
2. Eliminate poverty.
3. Avoid national debt.
4. Address legitimate needs of the poor.

The Hebrew mind could not grasp a concept of blessing without a tangible, as well as intangible, manifestation. The goodness of God was tied, in part, to having enough food, clothing, and shelter. The word "shalom" itself contained the concept of material blessing. Most of the earth's population today is desperate for this gospel.

STUDY HELP:

Themes to consider when studying and coloring economics in the bible: *Ethics and principles of finance, loans, agriculture, the worker, labor, the manager, inheritance, wages.*

The domain of economics reveals: **Jehovah Jireh, God our Provider**
The primary attribute of God revealed in economics: **Goodness**
God governs this domain through: **The laws of agriculture**
The color I used: **Green**

WORKING VOCATIONAL MISSIONS STATEMENT:

To develop an economy where needed goods and services are provided for the community along with gainful employment at a fair market price and wage. **Great issues include:** honest gain, enablement of the poor, integrity of the work force, stewardship of resources and community conscience.

NOTE TO ALL BELIEVERS:

We all deal with finances and material blessing, or the need of it. This is not a travesty; this is not a terrible diversion from more important things; this is God's plan for revealing Himself as Jehovah Jireh, the Lord of Goodness. So many want God's material blessing without understanding God's financial principles. God does want to bless us, but He wants to bless us in every area of our lives, not just provide us with material things. He wants us to be a blessing not just to be blessed. He wants to bless us in ways that make us more like Himself.

Do you know and live by God's financial principles? Can't answer that question? Don't beat yourself up; you have much company in the body of Christ globally. Do you want to know God's thinking about finance? Why not begin by reading His word with this theme in mind? I guarantee that God is ready and willing to disciple you in this area. You have to give Him the opportunity by being in His Word. You are a part of God's strategy for discipling your community and nation. Will you step up to the call?

A NOTE TO THE BUSINESS PROFESSIONAL:

If you are a banker, a business person, a laborer, a manager, a store owner, a stock broker or a ditch digger who provides goods and services for your community or nation in any way, you are part of God's plan to reveal Jehovah Jireh, God our Provider. The Bible has as much to say about finance and its purpose in blessing a people as any other subject in scripture including salvation. Most view business today as a means to make money and nothing more. In scripture, business is a means to make money and a great deal more. In scripture, it is about provision, about quality of life, about demonstrations of goodness and blessing. The Bible speaks about the worship of work and the Creator of work, about skill and craftsmanship and the work being worthy of the maker. The creature reveals the Creator in the quality of his work just as the Creator has revealed Himself in the quality of His work. Community responsibility and creative solutions reveal the goodness of God to every level of our society. You have a call of God on your life. Like Joseph you are part of God's revelation of His ability to provide all that is needed in abundance. You are part of His plan to reveal the quality of the workman. What would happen if every Christian in the world showed up for work on time? Performed at their absolute best? Set their sights on blessing the community and company rather than blessing themselves? What would happen if every Christian who owned a business asked, "What does our community really need and how can we provide that and make a profit?" rather than "Where can we make the most money?" Before we can begin to dream, we must know what God wants us to dream. In order to know that, we must understand what He has already taught us in His Word. Does something stir in your heart as you read this? Are you one called of God to begin saturating yourself with the mind of Christ and then to apply it in your life and work? You are part of God's strategy for discipling your nation.

CHAPTER 8
Science

"If you listen carefully to the voice of the Lord your God and do what is right in his eyes, if you pay attention to his commands and keep all his decrees, I will not bring on you any of the diseases I brought on the Egyptians, for I am the Lord, who heals you."

Exodus 15:26

"God saw all that he had made, and it was very good."

Genesis 1:31

George Washington Carver was a black American slave who used his great mind to pull himself from bondage, becoming one of America's greatest scientists. He held over 1,000 patents for the use of the peanut alone. Asked how he could think of 1,000 ways to use the peanut he replied that he held the peanut in his hand and said, "God, You made every seed bearing plant and You said they were good.[1] What did You make the peanut for?"

Virtually every astronaut who has ventured out into space, has returned to Earth talking about the Creator, awestruck by the magnificence of the cosmos. King David and King Solomon were not only great political leaders but loved science[2] and worshiped the Lord of Creation. For the Jews, creation was the first revelation of God. Paul said it is the material world which so eloquently reveals the invisible attributes of God that no one has an excuse for not seeing Him.[3] Paul argued with the mystics of

---

1. *Genesis 1:11-12*
2. *1 Kings 4:33*
3. *Romans 1:20*

his day that God is not only the God of the unseen world but also of the seen.[4] It could be argued that modern science as we know it came from the biblical view that God created everything there is and He created it with laws by which it works. The discovery and understanding of those laws can lead us to a better quality of life.

Today, however, many Christians loathe the discipline of science, thinking it is the battleground for disproving the existence of God. Others feel it is the lesser plane of the *material* and not as important as the *spiritual* realm. Some actually believe that it shows a lack of faith to search for and use scientific discovery. These ideas are a far cry from the teaching of the Old Testament, the fruit of the early church, and the root of both Jesus and Paul's messages. An understanding of the message of Christ not based in a clear biblical foundation of the material world is more Eastern and mystic than it is biblical.

As the gospel traveled the globe in the first 1800 years, it took the message of "cleanliness is next to godliness" with it. Improved sanitation and health accompanied the concept of salvation. The sanitation practices of the Jews in the black plagues of Europe were so superior that some thought they had "magic" arts, when, in fact, they were just continuing to practice what God had taught in the books of Moses. How does this compare with a "Christianized" southern Africa that is faced with near extinction because of disease? When some of the most important moral issues in the 21st Century are being asked in the realm of science, what does the near absence of a clear biblical view forewarn?

Let's begin to get an idea of what Moses was teaching:

Deuteronomy 23:9-14

9 When you are encamped against your enemies, keep away from everything impure.

10 If one of your men is unclean because of a nocturnal emission, he is to go outside the camp and stay there.

11 But as evening approaches he is to wash himself, and at sunset he may return to the camp.

12 Designate a place outside the camp where you can go to relieve yourself.

---

4. Colossians 1:16

13 As part of your equipment have something to dig with, and when you relieve yourself, dig a hole and cover up your excrement.
14 For the LORD your God moves about in your camp to protect you and to deliver your enemies to you. Your camp must be holy, so that he will not see among you anything indecent and turn away from you.

The scriptures are very down to earth and deal with life at its most basic. God deals with every dimension of His creation. Topics that make you and me uncomfortable are brought out for common sense understanding. This paragraph in Deuteronomy begins by dealing with nocturnal emissions. We will spare the men and skip that, and take up verses 12-14 which embarrasses everyone equally.

God has brought a great deliverance for more than two and a half million Jewish and alien slaves. They have experienced the miracle of the parting of the Red Sea. They have been eating miracle manna dropped from the sky on a daily basis. But they still needed to use the bathroom. You could say that this scene in the wilderness is the juxtaposition of God's teachings on the material world. He can invade our creation and do what none of us understands, but the daily norm is to work with the natural laws by which His creation was made to function. In these verses God is teaching basic hygiene.

The principles are fairly straightforward. **The community is to take responsibility to make provision for the daily need of all its citizens to urinate and defecate.** Secondly, **the citizens were to take personal responsibility to follow those guidelines.** Thirdly, **the waste was to be buried, as opposed to put in the water or left on top of the ground.** Fourthly, **the highest motivation possible is used – God's presence.** God, through Moses, is teaching public health. He is teaching sanitation and preventive health measures. The same God who did the impossible for His people by parting the Red Sea wants to teach them about His material world and the laws by which it works and He wants them to take responsibility for what they have learned. He is discipling them.

The Unclean Scriptures

When I was growing up, the "unclean" scriptures were taught allegorically as parallels for sin. I was glad that I hadn't lived in Old Testament days because walking through the streets shouting, "I am unclean," and spending a day outside the camp seemed fairly heavy treatment for minor infractions. From this allegorical treatment one got the notion that perhaps women were more unclean than men. I think this was drawn from the teaching that the mother was unclean for more days after the birth of a female child than after the birth of a male child.[5] This concept of women being more unclean became tied to the idea that Eve sinned first and, therefore, women are more prone to deception than men. Altogether, it was a grim scenario for women. However, the "unclean" scriptures are not allegories, they are historical and, more importantly, they were pragmatic guidelines given by God for community health.

This list of everything in the books of Moses, which would make you unclean, is quite revealing:
- Touching anything taken as spoils of war – Deut. 13:15-16
- Touching a human bone or grave – Num. 19:16
- Touching or being in the presence of a dead body – Num. 19:11
- Touching the discharge of a woman's period – Lev. 15:19,25
- Touching the discharge of a man's semen – Lev. 15:2,16
- Touching a man with a bodily discharge or his spit – Lev. 15:7-8
- Touching the bed or saddle touched by a man with a bodily discharge – Lev. 15:4,9
- Touching the nocturnal emission of a man – Deut. 23:10
- Touching human uncleanness, meaning urine or feces – Lev. 5:3
- Touching anything that touched any of these things – Lev. 7:21
- Touching the bed or chair that a woman with her period had touched – Lev. 15:20-21
- Touching or having a skin rash or outbreak on the skin – Lev. 13:2-3
- Touching or being exposed to mildew – Lev. 13:59
- Touching the blood of the sacrifices, if you were a priest – Num. 9:7

5. *Leviticus 12:5-12*

This list teaches us many things. First, it would appear that men are more likely to be unclean than women. Secondly, it seems that the poor priest is going to be the most unclean of all. Thirdly, none of this is about matters of the heart. It is about hygiene. God is teaching community health and prevention. When He says, "If you obey my laws you will have none of the diseases of the nations that surround you," He is not giving some formula for spiritual magic. He is teaching the prevention of transmittable diseases. And He is teaching this nearly 3,800 years before man will discover the germ. Not until the late 17th Century would we learn that there are invisible microbes and viruses that can be transmitted from one thing to another and cause disease. We would not understand clearly until the 1990's that the most viral transmitters of these invisible enemies are bodily fluids. It has taken the AIDS epidemic to reveal the extent of God's advanced understanding.

In 80 percent Christianized Africa, one out of four people, possibly even one out of three, are dying of AIDS. What would the statistic be if we added in all the other infectious diseases taking lives in that region? Where is the biblical influence that produced the healthiest, most scientifically advanced nations of the world? Remember, when the gospel came to Europe, Europeans were the "filthy pagans" that the advanced middle easterners weren't sure they wanted to mingle with. Where did antiseptic Switzerland, Germany, and Scandinavia come from? The minds and then the cultures of these peoples were transformed by a gospel that not only dealt with the conversion of the soul; the gospel they received was a gospel that dealt with all of life. It was a gospel that brought physical health as well as communion with God.

George Kinoti says, "Africa is plagued by numerous diseases. The most important are infectious diseases, which are both curable and preventable. An obvious example is malaria, which causes untold suffering in Africa and claims something like a million African lives a year. Malaria was once a major disease in the warmer parts of Europe and the U.S.A., but improvements in the living conditions led to its disappearance."[6] Two-thirds of the world is crying out for this gospel. Who will go? How will they know if someone does not tell them?

---

6. Kinoti, Ibid., page 7

Healing

A young mother of two children under four sat across from me in a New Zealand restaurant. She had just discovered that a dreaded lymphoma cancer had reappeared in her body just months after thinking she had been cured. The prognosis was not good. She looked at me and asked, "What do you think of healing?" Everything in me wanted to give popular charismatic or evangelical answers such as, "By His stripes you are healed; claim it and believe for it."[7] I wanted to give her the happy ending version, but I had been studying the Bible too long, and I knew that is not all that it teaches. Scripture does not teach that if we believe in Christ we will never get sick, that if we believe, we will be healed or that we will never die! You can find individual scriptures that would seem to mean that, but that is not what they mean because they make nonsense out of many other scriptures. Jesus died and Paul had a physical ailment that God did not heal even though Paul prayed three times.[8] Lazarus was raised from the dead and then he died again.

With a heavy heart I said to my friend that the Bible makes it clear that miracles are possible, but they are exceptions, not the rule. Miracles are spectacular interventions of God for His own unique purposes but they will never be the norm. We may always pray and ask God for healing, but the gospel message is that in death the enemy of our souls is finally defeated, not that we will not die. We live in a fallen world and disease is a reality. Our mortal bodies are wasting away. We can learn to live more wisely and deal with disease with prevention and cure, but we will all die. Then what is our hope? Our hope is that, through His death, Christ has overcome the evil one. At the very moment that Satan feels he has conquered us, the point of death, we are given an immortal body not corrupted by sin. The cross has removed the sting of death, not death itself. Job reveals to us that the enemy of God can sorely try us with crisis and illness, but Job also reveals that Satan cannot take our life when we belong to God. The issue is more *when* will we die, not *if* we will die.

The thinking of many Christians today is that there should be no suffering, there should be no death, we should have heaven now. Quoting Dr. Kinoti again, "religion...enables many to evade reality. Chris-

---

7. *Isaiah 53:5*
8. *2 Corinthians 12:8*

81

tians...sometimes use their faith as a narcotic to evade the pain, the ugliness, the difficulties, the concrete reality of the world in which we find ourselves."[9] The author is speaking specifically about African believers. But this is not only an African problem. This is one of the great problems in evangelical, pentecostal, and charismatic thinking in the last century and a half. We have drifted towards a belief that salvation delivers us from living in the material world. And it does not.

As I left the restaurant with my suffering friend I longed to say something that would comfort, and that was true. I put my arm around her and said, "Here is what I do know. If you live, you will be pure gold through this trial. If you die you will go into His presence and be perfected into His likeness. Either way, you cannot lose!" The week I was preparing this chapter I attended her funeral...knowing I had given her the comfort of His Word.

Worship And The Material World

All through scripture, creation draws the hearts of God's people to Him. David was stunned by the God who created the innumerable stars. Solomon tried to grasp understanding of the seasons and the God who created the rotation of the planets. Paul expected man to understand the existence and attributes of God simply by considering the creation around him. Creation captures God's awesomeness. In the era of Cathedral building, Europeans were mystified by the nature of space. They could not yet define the molecular structure of all things, and so air was mysterious and awesome. They incorporated this into their worship by getting architects and engineers to invent new building technology to convey the awe and wonder of God's creation in their cathedrals. They understood that science and worship could work hand in hand. Millions still visit these great monuments every year.

God is not at war with His material world. Science is, of all the domains, the most limited because the scientist cannot discover anything that God has not created. Certainly scientists can have theories that are not based in fact. But scientists cannot create new laws or new truths in the cosmos; they can only discover them. Today many Christians be-

---

9. *Kinoti, Ibid., page 3*

lieve, or at least behave as if by virtue of our faith, we are alienated from all science. This can be a grave danger. In the 16th Century the church and science were at odds with each other. Galileo and others had begun to postulate that the world was not flat but round. The theology of the day was built around a flat earth concept, and it supported the idea that heaven was up, and hell was down, and that man and the earth were at the center of the universe. The first proponent of this concept of a round globe was executed for heresy, teaching against the doctrines of the church. The second, Galileo himself, was put under house arrest.

Of course, in this instance, science was right and the theological interpretation of the day was wrong. God knew the truth all along. He was not thrown by our discovery. Science's discovery of some fact in His universe does not destroy the validity of scripture or challenge God's truth. This discovery simply led to a clearer understanding of what God meant by man being the center of the universe. It created the possibility that man was central to God's plan, but not necessarily central in cosmic geography. We did not yet know that *up* and *down* are relative terms relating to gravity. What these concepts mean outside our planet is quite another issue. God is not shaken by scientific discovery. He is not alienated from *His* material world; He uses it to reveal Himself and man is still discovering Him in it.

When I saw the Hubble telescope's pictures of the birth and death of stars, I was awestruck! The color, the power, the majesty in the creation of just one tiny star! Explosive plumes millions of miles high. Who cannot worship the God of creation when they see and discover such things? I was humbled to think that I live in the first generation that God has graced with such a view of what He has made, the awe of His power, the beauty of His universe in every detail. King David was overwhelmed by the innumerable stars. He saw God revealed in the shear scope of what he could see. The Hubble telescope was aimed at a black spot at the end of the handle of the Big Dipper. This spot was ten times blacker than anything we can see with the naked eye. The telescope viewed this black spot for ten days, absorbing light from deep space. When astronomers looked at the picture that the telescope sent back, they counted ten galaxies, all larger than ours, in the one black spot. Who cannot worship at the thought of His grandeur? Who cannot marvel at the Creator God? And yet today, with split thinking being the norm amongst Christians, if you heard of the Hubble telescope's discoveries at all, it was in the light of how the money could have been used for evangelism.

Summary

Are you beginning to get the picture of what we have lost in scripture? Are you seeing the tragedy of keeping God so boxed in? What else is God going to reveal to us in His universe? What other advanced understanding of the material world is He waiting to impart to us for the prevention of disease? God is the same yesterday, today and forever. God has not changed; we Christians have lost our understanding of God. He wants to restore us, to revive us through the revelation of Himself in the material world. Will we let Him?

We have looked at one small passage dealing with sanitation. There is so much more: teaching about ecology and our responsibility to steward His creation, about cures, about the priestly role in primary health care, about the pharmaceutical properties of plants. When you finish His study in the Bible you must conclude that God loves science.

STUDY HELP:

Themes to consider when studying and coloring science in scripture: *health, nature, hygiene, medicine, engineering, technology, ecology, animal kingdom.*

The domain of science reveals: **The Creator**

The primary attributes of God revealed in science: **Order and power**

God governs this domain through: **The laws of nature**

The color I used: **Blue**

WORKING VOCATIONAL MISSIONS STATEMENT:

To discover and use God's laws for the blessing of all people, pursuing a higher standard of living, better health, and better stewardship of all God's natural resources. **Great issues include:** Prevention of disease, discovery, and stewardship.

NOTE TO ALL BELIEVERS:

God is not afraid of science or discovery. Neither should you and I be. For me, a balanced approach to biblical healing is:
- Confess all known sin.
- Bind the enemy.
- Do everything medically known that may be helpful.
- Pray for a miracle.
- Put yourself in the loving hands of the Father; He knows best.

I believe I can support all of this from the Word of God. I would ask God to reveal to His science professionals a cure, just as He revealed preventives of infectious disease to Israel. Which do you think is the greater lasting witness: a miracle for an individual or a cure for everyone? Perhaps we cannot fairly ask that question as both reveal God. Are you praying for *both* revelations – miracles and cures – for the nations?

Are you prepared to refuse skepticism about all science and let God speak to you through what He is allowing us to discover? Man is fallen and tends to corrupt anything that can be corrupted. Of course, cloning could lead to trying to duplicate humans. But cloning and DNA research could also lead to a cure for many common diseases. Can we not see this discovery as the hand of God extended to us in mercy? The story of the tower of Babel is often used to discuss the evils of technology. But the sin of Babel is really political imperialism; the tower was just the symbol. What we see in scripture is that when the technology got out of hand, God destroyed it by confusing the people.

What is the point for us then? Don't fret about new discoveries and developments. If they threaten God's plan, He will deal with them. If He is allowing the discovery, our question should be, "God, how do you want to use this to glorify Yourself?" Christians did this with the discovery of movable type and printing and, consequently, are still the largest publishers of printed matter. But, we tend to push aside the technology of the internet as demonic. What has changed? God? No, we Christians have. Alienation from discovery which God is allowing can only result in lessening the purposes of God. Let's work again to receive the whole council of God's Word in this wonderful arena of science and His material revelation.

A NOTE TO THE SCIENCE PROFESSIONAL:

When I spoke on this topic in Urbana, Illinois a sanitation engineer, whose brother was a missionary, came up to me in tears. All his life the work of his brother had been applauded as a *spiritual* calling. This brother had been made to feel less important because of his *unspiritual* profession. He said to me, "No one has ever told me that what I do is important to God, too." I was in 40 percent[10] Christian Togo some time ago and saw that people had taken to spray painting, "Ne urine pas ici!" "Do not urinate here!" on the walls around their houses and businesses. I thought "Great! Half the gospel of sanitation." But who will teach them the other half...where should they urinate? Several summers ago a large tribe of pentecostal Gypsies came to Switzerland to hold healing and evangelistic services. They pitched a giant tent very near my home and used the parking lot of our forest running and exercise course for their cars and trailers. The two small toilets of the exercise course and their trailer toilets were obviously not adequate for the needs of such a large group. As the week's evangelistic services went on, the forest trails became increasingly littered with feces and toilet paper. At first, you may be irate and think this is just stupid, but we need to be more compassionate. You see, these dear people had been taught that Jesus saves and Jesus heals, but they had never been taught what the Bible teaches about sanitation.

As a professional in the science domain, you have a high calling. You are the discoverers and stewards of God's material creation. You are called to know Him in a special way as He reveals Himself in the things He has made. You are called to use that knowledge to bless individuals,

---

10. Johnstone, Ibid.

communities, and nations. No calling in God's Kingdom is second rate. No domain of revelation is more or less important than another; they are all created by God to reveal Himself. The pastor has one job and you have another. The missionary prays to be shown worthy of his calling and so should you. God makes His "cause and effect" relationship with man most evident in this domain. He uses His natural laws to humble us and reveal His awesome power and wisdom. Are you one of God's George Washington Carvers? Are you called to hold in your hand something of God's creation and say, "God, you made this and you said it was good. Why did you make this peanut, atom, DNA cell, planet, bug, tree?" The sky is not the limit. God's revelation of Himself stretches to the farthest reaches of the cosmos. How far is that? Perhaps He will use you to reveal that to us and strike us with awe again. You are part of God's strategy for discipling all nations.

CHAPTER 9
Church

"The Lord had said to Moses: 'You must not count the tribe of Levi or include them in the census of the other Israelites. Instead, appoint the Levites to be in charge of the tabernacle of the Testimony...'"

Numbers 1:48-50

"The reason I left you in Crete was that you might straighten out what was left unfinished and appoint elders in every town, as I directed you."

Titus 1:5

"Here is a trustworthy saying: If anyone sets his heart on being an overseer, he desires a noble task."

1 Timothy 3:1

All the Israelites were Jews, but not all Jews were priests. Under God's direction, Moses chose Joshua to continue political leadership while Aaron and the Levitical tribe are given the priesthood. From the earliest days in the wilderness God made it clear that government and the priesthood were two different and distinct institutions, both with clear Kingdom purpose and function. This concept of an ecclesiastical structure with an independent function, apart from the overall function of the body of believers, has been hard for Protestants to grasp since Luther nailed his treatise to the Wittenberg door in 1517. But understanding the institution of the church is foundational to understanding the unique, God-given functions of all the domains in society.

Today we use the words *priesthood, believer, body of Christ,* and *church* rather interchangeably. All Christians are priests, believers, the church, and part of the body of Christ. For clarity in this study, we need to differentiate between the people, the building, and the individual believers who work full-time in a particular function such as pastors, missionaries, and evangelists.

When Luther highlighted that we are all part of the priesthood of believers, he did not mean that there was no structure or leadership to the Church. He meant that we do not need a "priest" to represent us to God. Because of the work of the cross and Christ in our lives, we are all now free to come before God ourselves. Under Luther's leadership and those who followed him, a church structure was created with pastors, elders, and deacons. As believers, we all are encouraged to fellowship on Sundays. However, some of us go to work on Monday at the same building where we went to church. The rest of the believers go to work on Monday in some other important role within their community.

All of Israel was taught to be holy, but the Levitical tribe (the priests) were to model holiness to the rest of the nation. The book of Leviticus focuses, in the main, on their unique role as an ecclesiastical institution.

Appointment Of The Priests

In Numbers 1:47-50; the selection of the priesthood is a completely different process than that for choosing political leaders. In Deuteronomy 1:13, God instructs Moses to have the people choose their political representatives. In the development of the priesthood, God made the selection Himself. **The anointing to minister in the ecclesiastical order comes directly from God.**[1]

The priests were not chosen on the basis of personal merit.[2] God made priests of the entire Levitical tribe. This is not to say that character and virtue did not matter; scripture is clear that God desired a holy priesthood. But God did not choose the virtuous elite; He chose an entire tribe filled with every level of character and virtue. We have to stop and ponder: What was God's point in selecting this way? Was

---

1. *Numbers 3:12*
2. *Numbers 3:12; 18:6-7*

He emphasizing that no one is holy? That He was able to make anyone holy? That holiness only belongs to Him and no one is innately worthy of representing His holiness? We don't know all the possible answers, but this fact is clear: God sovereignly selected ecclesiastical ministers.

The priests responsible for the most holy things were not given carts in the wilderness.[3] As Israel moved around the wilderness for 40 years, they began to acquire things. Carts were divided out to each of the tribes. The Levites were given very few carts and the Kohathites, who carried the holiest implements of the Tabernacle, were given none at all. They were required to carry the Tabernacle and all of the utensils of worship and sacrifice on their backs. Over and over again God encouraged them to be satisfied with their unique inheritance in the Lord. The result of not being given carts, and additionally being required to carry the Tabernacle, put a limitation on the priesthood's ability to acquire wealth. That did not mean that they were to live in destitution. However, it did limit their potential for financial power among their people.

The priesthood was to receive its provision from offerings and was given small plots of land for farming in each of the tribal territories.[4] These directions made the priesthood uniquely dependent on the people to whom they ministered. They had all authority to speak for God and to represent Him to the community, but they did not have all authority. God limited their financial and political power in the community.

The priesthood was not given territorial land.[5] On leaving Egypt there were thirteen tribes in Israel. Both of Joseph's sons, Ephraim and Manasseh, were given tribal status by their grandfather Jacob. As they formed government and began to prepare for their future in Canaan, God made it clear that only twelve tribes would have territorial or tribal land. The thirteenth tribe, the Levites, would have their inheritance in God. This meant that the priests would never need to form a government, as the other tribes must. This meant that the Levites did not need to develop an army as all the other tribes were commanded to do. The Levites were to be split among the other twelve tribes and territories and be God's priestly representation to all of them.

---

3. *Numbers 7:9*
4. *Numbers 18:21,24; 35:2-3; Deuteronomy 18:1; Joshua 14:4*
5. *Numbers 18:20; Deuteronomy 12:12; Joshua 14:4*

The priests were the first primary health care givers.[6] Until the scientific community developed, the priesthood took care of the primary heath care needs of the people. If they had an infection, they were to go to the priest. He was to put them in quarantine and inspect them again some days later. The priests taught the dietary laws, which were about nutrition and health. The priests prayed and took the needs of the people to God. The priests offered sacrifices for their sins.

The result of this was that the priests had to constantly deal in the pragmatic, material world of God's laws of nature and in the unseen world of God's sovereign intervention. God did not allow the Levites to develop a mindset that the seen and the unseen world were secular and sacred, one under God and one under man. Every day, as His representatives, they had to minister to the practical, physical needs, as well as the needs of the inner man.

The prophets anointed Kings but they did not appoint them.[7] This is most clear in the process of Israel first wanting a king. Israel goes to Samuel, the prophet of the day, to consult God. Samuel consults God and God says that this is not a good idea. But the priests and prophets do not control this decision. The people do and, finally, Israel decides that they will have a king in spite of the fact that this is not God's desire. God then tells Samuel to go and anoint Saul and pray for him, because if Israel insists on having a king, Saul is the man God wants them to choose. But, still, Saul is not officially "appointed" King when he is anointed. Only the people can give Saul authority to rule. Saul wasn't appointed king until "all the people went to Gilgal and confirmed Saul as King in the presence of the Lord."[8] Virtually this same process took place in the selection of David and Solomon. The Levitical tribe had political influence, but it did not have political control. The authority of the priesthood, like the authority in every other domain, was limited.

The confusion of political authority and priestly authority in scripture resulted in severe consequences. Two examples of this stand out. The first is the incident that we are so familiar with in 1 Samuel 13:1-13. Saul had been to war and won a victory. He and his troops were waiting on the battlefield for the prophet Samuel to come and offer the sacrifice to God

---

6. *Leviticus 13 & 14*
7. *1 Samuel 9:16; 10:1*
8. *1 Samuel 11:14-15*

before they could return home. Samuel was delayed and Saul grew impatient. Finally, Saul decided he would offer the sacrifice. When Samuel arrived, he asked Saul, "What have you done? Today your Kingdom is taken from you." Saul was not satisfied to be given political leadership by God. He wanted more power. He wanted priestly authority over the people as well, and he lost his kingdom for confusing the two God-given domains. We find a similar confusion in the life of David.

David loved God and he loved worship. He used his political power to help build up the priesthood, the Tabernacle and, ultimately, the Temple. This support did not seem to be criticized in scripture. However, on one occasion David confused his role as king and the role of the priest. The consequences were very serious. David had been appointed king in Israel and had successfully conquered Jerusalem and defeated the Philistines. An invading army had taken the Ark of the Covenant. In 2 Samuel 6:1, David decided it was time to take back the stolen ark. "David again brought together out of Israel chosen men, thirty thousand in all." David approached this task as a military endeavor. He used the might of the army and his political authority to bring the ark back and God could not bless it. "When they came to the threshing-floor of Nachon, Uzzah reached out and took hold of the ark of God, because the oxen stumbled." When the man who tried to steady the ark dropped dead, David knew that God was not with this venture. He cried out, "How can the ark of the Lord ever come to me?" (2 Samuel 6:9) David stored the ark in the house of Obed-Edom and returned to Jerusalem in defeat. But the story did not end there. In the same chapter, David went again to retrieve the ark, but this time he went with the Levites who offered sacrifices every six steps. This time the ark was carried, as it would have been carried by the priest, as Moses commanded in Numbers 4:15 and Deuteronomy 10:8, and as Solomon understood in 1 Kings 8:3-4. David wore a linen ephod of worship, not battle clothes, and the people went in a procession of worship and praise, not military might. God had answered David's question of how to move the ark in 1 Chronicles 15:2, and He made it clear that He gave that authority to the priests, not the king.

The prophets were advisors to the king, but they were not kings. God did not give all authority in His kingdom to any one domain or person. The priesthood had authority, but not all authority. The political authorities in Israel had authority as well, but it was different from the priests'. Under God, they had to work together in a system of checks and balances. **All of Israel was to be holy, but the priests were to be models of holiness to the community.** The book of Leviticus contains instructions primarily for the priesthood regarding how they are to live and how they are to conduct themselves. They had a unique role in the community, but they did not have the only God-given role.

Secular Vs. Sacred

Our split thinking between the secular and sacred is probably more revealed in our thinking about the ecclesiastical order than any other domain. Today it is common among Christians to think that if you are really "spiritual," really "obedient" to God, you will be a pastor, missionary, or evangelist. Many Christians feel that all other vocations are less important. The end result is that the majority of Christians today are sitting in pews with no idea of what God has called them to do, expecting the pastor and church leadership to do everything. This was never God's intent. In God's design, every believer has a role to play in reaching and teaching the community. The "priestly" role was unique, specific, and just one of many roles.

Jesus understood the importance of keeping each domain in its proper place. When he saw that the moneychangers had moved their business inside the walls of the Temple, He threw them out. He did not say that money changing was wrong. He said that it had no place in His father's Temple. He emphasized the role of this ecclesiastical meeting place as a "house of prayer."[9]

If we are to see "every creature reached" and "every nation discipled," we must learn again the specific role of the "ecclesiastical" institution and how it relates to the calling and authority of each of the other domains.

---

9. *Matthew 21:12-13; Mark 11:15-17; Luke 19:45-46*

STUDY HELP:

Themes to consider when studying and coloring the ecclesiastical order in scripture: *religious rituals, prayer, offerings, sacrifices, priests, worship, tithes, feasts, idolatry, covenants, the Tabernacle, the Temple.*
The domain of church reveals: **The Great High Priest**
The primary attributes of God revealed in the church: **Holiness and Mercy**
God governs this domain through: **His sovereign choice and anointing**
The color I used: **Gold**

WORKING VOCATIONAL MISSION STATEMENT:

The ecclesiastical order is called to represent God to the people, and the people to God, providing for the discipleship of all believers in the whole nature and character of God and His Word applied to the work and walk of faith, to facilitate the expression of that faith in the worship and sacraments of the church, and to be a moral model of God's absolute standards of truth. **Great issues include:** Calling society to accountability to the word of God.

A NOTE TO ALL BELIEVERS:

Many Christians are sitting in the world's churches today wishing they had a "real" calling to be a pastor or a missionary. They feel they would be more "spiritual" in these callings. Many feel that they are not called to be pastors or church workers because they are less worthy. All of this is the by-product of "split thinking." It results from the idea that the "secular" is bad and the "sacred" is good. This is not biblical thinking. If you are called by God to give your working life to family, or government, or business, or science, or teaching, or arts, or communication, you are not called to a lesser vocation than ministry within the church structure. You are called to a different vocation than ministry. Your calling is equally from God, equally vital to that of those called to serve the church. Discipling the nations is a saturation strategy of getting the truth into the fiber of every layer of society through the lives of every believer.

For too long we have put all the weight of the work of God on the shoulders of the pastor or church worker. It is time for us to bear our own weight. What has God called you to do in society? It is time to get grateful for the doors God has opened for our life work and to be determined to carry out our job as a calling unto God Himself.

A NOTE TO THE MINISTRY PROFESSIONAL:

Some of you in the ministry today will be relieved by what I have said in this chapter, and some of you will be threatened. The pastor and missionary in the 20th Century have been expected by many to be all things to all men. For some, when we discuss "discipling the nations," they think all the work will be their responsibility. Some are hoping it will be. Whatever your perspective, I encourage us all to pursue God for a clear revelation of a working job description for ourselves and for each of our followers. Only when the 80 percent of the body of Christ not called to the ministry of the church are released to do what God has called them to do, can those of us in full-time ministry in the church begin to focus on our call.

Some in the ministry have asked, "Why are we out there talking about discipling the nations instead of doing it?" I am not sure what they mean, however, this I do know: it is the responsibility of the "priesthood" to teach and clarify for the body of Christ its job. It is not our job to start businesses and banks; it is our job to teach and disciple business people and bankers in the full counsel of God as it relates to their calling. It is not our job to run the government and write the constitutions; it is our job to teach those who are called of God into those vocations how to carry out their responsibilities in accordance with the Word of God. It is not our job to be the father to the family, but to teach the father God's way of fathering. This is so clear and simple that I am sometimes flabbergasted by all the confusion. The only explanation I have for the volume of confusion is that we have so bought into the secular/sacred split we are unable to conceive of the call of God on those outside the "ecclesiastical" institution. We are not to bring all the domains under the church structure; we are to send the body of Christ away on Sunday prepared to be Christ's ambassadors of wisdom in their individual and specific domain callings. If we are to launch a generation prepared again to see qualitative differences in not only their lives, but in their communities, we must reintroduce an adequate theology of the laity, as well as of the "priesthood." The institution of the church has a pivotal role in discipling the nations if we understand what our role is and is not.

CHAPTER 10
Family

*"Honor your father and your mother, as the Lord your God has
commanded you, so that you may live long and that it may go well
with you in the land the Lord your God is giving you."*

Deuteronomy 5:16

*"Take to heart all the words I have solemnly declared to you this day,
so that you may command your children to obey carefully all the
words of this law. They are not just idle words for
you – they are your life."*

Deuteronomy 32:46-47

Of all the domains in the Kingdom of God, family is probably the
most discussed and studied by Christians. We base political platforms on
"family values," and yet the divorce rate continues to climb...50 percent,
verging on 60 percent in some regions, with no significant difference between the Christian and non-Christian population. Why? Can the power
of God save our souls but not restore our families?

Over this last decade of coloring the scriptures by domains in order to
understand God's thinking in every arena of life, nothing has more impacted my thinking than God's view of family, its influence, and its role
in community at large. I do not have one key scripture to study here, but
thousands address marriage, children, in-laws, conflicts, sexual conduct,
inheritance laws, family and finance, family and justice, education and
much, much more.

We Learn 80 Percent Of What We Know In The Home

Like communication and education, the domain of family provides the warp to the government's and church's weave. Family's influence touches everyone and everything. It is said that by the time we are four we will have learned/established 80 percent of our view of life. By the time we enter school we know whether we are good or bad, whether the world is safe or dangerous, whether we are bright or stupid and whether other people are to be feared or trusted. We have learned a life strategy of asking questions or building defences. We already know whether challenges are exciting or dangerous. Uninterrupted, we will continue to evaluate all of life and the world we live in through that grid of reality. In our modern Christian terminology you could say that we have most of our worldview in place before we ever leave home for school. To say it another way, in our first four years of life, parents and the home environment will give us the definition of reality that we'll use all our lives.

An impressive example of the power of that home influence is the cultural landscape of New Zealand. This small island nation's population is divided between indigenous Maori peoples and immigrant Europeans. In many ways, New Zealand's daily life is integrated in schools, shops, transportation, news and mass media and entertainment, dress, and sports. However, the worldview/culture of the Maori and European in New Zealand are as different as if they still lived nearly half a world apart. How can this be? Where are these values and views of reality learned? In the home! From the family! With almost no intentionality.

In an age when we focus on almost everything but the family – movies, T.V., music, school, friends – God puts His sights directly on the family as the most important influence in society. The biblical overview leaves you with an overwhelming sense that, for God, family is sacred and the most important building block of all He has created. The family is responsible for His most cherished of all attributes: Love! No wonder the distortion in this domain is so great.

Song Of Songs

Few topics get an entire book in scripture; love and the anticipation of marriage is one exception. When God highlights something with such attention we should do the same. Song of Songs celebrates the exhilarating highs and lows of emotional love and the anticipation of its physical expression in marriage. In a day when Christians are viewed as having a diminished view of sex, God clearly thinks it is a good idea. The Song of Songs is a celebration of the joy, comfort and pleasure of marriage. It is not only celebrated by the bride and groom, but by their friends and the community at large. The message could not be clearer on God's side: Love is good. Marriage is good. Sex is good. And family is good.

Genesis chapters one and two set the stage for the importance of men and women working together. God says that it takes both the male and female to reveal the image of God and that He blessed "them" and family as His primary strategies for filling the earth with the revelation of Himself.

Genesis 1:27-28

So God created man in his own image, in the image of God he created him; male and female he created them. God blessed them and said to them, "Be fruitful and increase in number; fill the earth and subdue it. Rule over the fish of the sea and the birds of the air and over every living creature that moves on the ground.

By chapter three we can see that the enemy of God has another plan which results, first of all, in a separation of God and man and, secondly, in hostility and distrust between man and woman. The devastating results can still be seen today as God's sacred creation of family remains a primary battleground in every society in the world. Divorced men are eight times more likely to suffer mental illness. Broken homes produce greater numbers of sociopaths with little, if any, regard for community. Financial ruin and poverty follow divorce and the next generation is maimed before they ever have a chance at life. That's the bad news about family. What's the good news? What was God's intent in creation?

As we move through Genesis, we see that God highlights the origins of the cosmos, the individual, family, tribes, and finally, the origins of nations. Our Western syncretism of the idol of individualism has nearly blinded our biblical scholarship to the importance of the family and community unit. Most of God's attributes cannot be seen or taught in isolation. The idea that living completely alone would be paradise seems idyllic, but it is sterile. You cannot express love, justice, relationship, generosity, and wisdom alone on an island. God's most wonderful ideas and characteristics are revealed in how we live together and we begin learning of all these attributes in our family.

Family: The Root Of All Culture

As we follow the development of man through the Genesis narrative we see that individual traits become multiplied and strengthened in families. Then, as families grow, those same traits become amplified into cultural, tribal, and finally, national traits. Take, for example, Abraham's tendency to be manipulative, and sometimes actually dishonest, especially when it came to women in the family. In Genesis chapter 12, Abraham deceives the pharaoh about the nature of his relationship with Sarah in order to protect himself. In spite of God's promises in chapter 15, Abraham allows himself to be talked into seeking an heir through a concubine and so begins the story of the ancestors of Ishmael (Chapter 16). In chapter 20, Abraham is again faced with danger and lies to Abimelech about his wife. Isaac is born and marries Rebekah and carries on the family trait in chapter 26, again lying about the nature of his relationship with his wife in order to protect himself from danger. Jacob enters the picture and, with the help of his mother, deceives Isaac as to his identity in order to steal Esau's blessing. Fleeing, Jacob goes to his family in Paddan Aram and meets his match in his uncle and future father-in-law, Laban. These two spend twenty-one years trying to get the better of each other over the issue of Rachael. Are you beginning to see the pattern and escalation? As Jacob flees Laban and resettles his small tribe in Shechem, personal character flaws, which have grown into destructive family patterns, explode into tribal disaster. In chapter 34 Jacob's daughter is violated by the Prince of Shechem who is remorseful and actually loves and is loved by Dinah. Jacob's sons, in the name of family honor and no small amount of acquired wealth, deceived and then murdered every male in the Shechemite tribe.

A character trait has run its full course into cultural identity and ends in genocide. This trait of treachery turns in on the family and Joseph, taking Israel into Egypt and 400 years of exile and slavery. Joseph, on the other hand, is given opportunity to respond in deceit when he is unjustly abused by Potiphar and his wife, the cup bearer, the baker, and finally, with great temptation, his own brothers. But he refuses to deceive and is used of God to save his family, his tribe, and his host nation from great famine. Of course God is teaching us many things in Genesis, but certainly one of the major themes is the influence of individuals on families, families on communities, and finally, communities on tribes. Discipling nations begins in the home!

Family: First Line Of Defense – Values (Education)

One of the first things that struck me in the study of family was the emphasis given to time together with parents and children and how that time was to be used. Over and over again you will read phrases like: "when you walk, lie down, get up,"[1] "when you sit",[2] "write them on the door frames of your houses and on your gates."[3] These are instructions for parents in teaching their children God's thoughts on all of life, and modeling how these principles are lived out in daily life. Not only is parental responsibility and authority reinforced in scripture, but government or church involvement in the primary discipleship of children is almost completely absent.

We hear great complaint about our schools, our churches, and our entertainment industry's lack of responsibility to give children good values, but God puts the greatest weight of responsibility on the parents. I do not

---

1. *Deuteronomy 6:7*
2. *Deuteronomy 11:19*
3. *Deuteronomy 6:9*

want to argue *for* immorality, violence, and drugs. However, when we blame the gun, the entertainment industry, the government, the schools, and the streets for children's problems, we are not focusing on what God focuses on. In essence we are saying, "Make the world safe so that my child will be safe." This is far from the biblical view of reality. God says, "In order for your children to be safe in an unsafe world, teach and model what they need to know and understand. Sin is real and we are surrounded by destruction. Teach your children to choose good over evil!"

Scripture assumes that this will take time and that parents and children are doing things together and using opportunities to discuss how God's view of reality relates to our everyday living. Can we really expect children to take these values seriously if they do not see them modeled and revered in their parents' lives? By the time they go to school, children know from the way their parents have lived whether honesty, justice, integrity, courage, and other character traits are important or not. Of course school, teachers, pastors, Sunday School, friends and culture can have a dramatic impact, but the home is still the formative influence and, in God's eyes, clearly the most important. It is the grid of reality the child will use to interpret all other influences in life.

Family: First Line Of Defense – Morality

If we would just obey one of God's ten commandments, "You shall not commit adultery"[4] we would virtually eliminate:

- **Incest:** In some areas of South Africa incest accounts for 70 per cent of all sexual abuse cases.[5]
- **Pedophilia:** An estimated ten million are involved in exploitation for profit of children.[6]
- **Abortion:** 77 percent of abortions in England and Wales in 2004 of single women.[7]

---

4. *Exodus 20:14*
5. *"Jobus Long Walk to Comfort" by Neville Josie on http://www.unicef.org/southafrica/reallives_2141.html; "Blamed For A Crime Committed Against Me" by James Hall http://www.UNICEF/southafrica/resources_1846.html*
6. *End Child Prostitution, Child Pornography and Trafficking of Children for Sexual Purposes (ECPAT - www.ecpat.org)*
7. *CARE, UK*

- **Sexually** transmitted diseases: Syphilis is up 1500 percent in the UK and rising.[8]
- **Rape:** Over one quarter of all rapes in the UK are committed against children under 16 years of age.[9]

Overwhelming, isn't it? Today we, Christians included, seem to be shocked by sexual immorality. In the Bible, God seems to take it for granted. Undeterred, scripture teaches that human beings will have sex with just about anyone and anything. How else do we explain the long lists in Deuteronomy and Leviticus on who (and what) not to have sex with? Somewhere we've picked up the idea that sexual morality is the norm and deviance is the exception. God seems to think otherwise in both the Old and New Testament.

Look at just this one chapter:

Leviticus 18:5-24

5 Keep my decrees and laws, for the man who obeys them will live by them. I am the LORD.

6 "No-one is to approach any close relative to have sexual relations. I am the LORD.

7 "Do not dishonor your father by having sexual relations with your mother. She is your mother; do not have relations with her.

8 "Do not have sexual relations with your father's wife; that would dishonor your father.

9 "Do not have sexual relations with your sister, either your father's daughter or your mother's daughter, whether she was born in the same home or elsewhere.

10 "Do not have sexual relations with your son's daughter or your daughter's daughter; that would dishonor you.

11 "Do not have sexual relations with the daughter of your father's wife, born to your father; she is your sister.

12 "Do not have sexual relations with your father's sister; she is your father's close relative.

13 "Do not have sexual relations with your mother's sister, because

---

8. *http://news.bbc.CO.UK/1/hi/programmes/panorama/4339264.stm*
9. *End Child Prostitution, Child Pornography and Trafficking of Children for Sexual Purposes (ECPAT - www.ecpat.org)*

she is your mother's close relative.

14 "Do not dishonor your father's brother by approaching his wife to have sexual relations; she is your aunt.

15 "Do not have sexual relations with your daughter-in-law. She is your son's wife; do not have relations with her.

16 "Do not have sexual relations with your brother's wife; that would dishonor your brother.

17 "Do not have sexual relations with both a woman and her daughter. Do not have sexual relations with either her son's daughter or her daughter's daughter; they are her close relatives. That is wickedness.

18 "Do not take your wife's sister as a rival wife and have sexual relations with her while your wife is living.

19 "Do not approach a woman to have sexual relations during the uncleanness of her monthly period.

20 "Do not have sexual relations with your neighbor's wife and defile yourself with her.

21 "Do not give any of your children to be sacrificed to Molech, for you must not profane the name of your God. I am the LORD.

22 "Do not lie with a man as one lies with a woman; that is detestable.

23 "Do not have sexual relations with an animal and defile yourself with it. A woman must not present herself to an animal to have sexual relations with it; that is a perversion.

24 "Do not defile yourselves in any of these ways, because this is how the nations that I am going to drive out before you became defiled."

God could have saved an enormous amount of time by just shortening this to "don't have sex with anyone but your spouse." But God is defining what He means by the word *adultery* and He is emphasizing the destruction of immorality, especially in the family. We must not think this means sexuality outside the family is not a sin, but God is stressing that sexual immorality within the family has multiple victims – the two engaged in sexual conduct, and the families that surround them.

Today, we in the religious community, seem to highlight the destructiveness of prostitution and homosexuality while virtually ignoring marital adultery, sexual abuse, and incest, which are all rampant. I have never heard a sermon on incest or rape and its impact on family and society. I am not arguing that we should condone any destructive sexual behavior. I am simply saying that we have ceased to view the severity of these issues from God's perspective. We take adultery and divorce fairly lightly, even in the church.

How can we raise children who will be able to withstand the sexual onslaughts of the world if they do not see morality modeled in the home? How can we have bold, confident children when so many family secrets send a message that is contrary to what God says? How can we be shocked by what God takes for granted? And if we don't teach our own children to love and respect their bodies and to view sex as a Godly and sacred act in the faithful covenant of marriage at home, then who will teach them? Please don't think they won't figure sex out until "it is time." As we attack government and school programs that teach sexual behavior, let us remember that God has given parents the responsibility to model and teach that value to their children. If they don't... someone will. God knows who should.

Family: First Line Of Defense – Provision

In both the Old and New Testament, family is the first line of protection against poverty and economic ruin. The definition of *destitute* and who should feed the destitute was one of the early debates in the Church. Paul makes it clear in 1 Timothy 5 that if the poor have family, the family is to take care of them. Only if they have no other alternative, i.e. work or family, is the church to give assistance. The custom of the Pharisees was to tithe everything, even the herbs in their kitchen. Jesus rebuked them for tithing mint and leaving their parents without financial help.[10]

The book of Ruth recounts the story of the widow Naomi and her widowed daughter-in-law, Ruth. Refugees, childless, and without recourse in a foreign land, they return to Israel and the town of their family origin. Here they find aid by gleaning in the fields of their closest relative, Boaz, who takes his right as "kindred redeemer," marries Ruth,[11] and brings her and Naomi into his home to care for them. What a wonderful concept,

---

10. *1 Timothy 5:8; Matthew 23:23*
11. *Ruth 4*

"kindred redeemer!" God's first line of responsibility for those in financial need was the family, not the church, community or government.

Jewish culture, in general, still functions this way. I have traveled to nearly half of the world's nations and it is very rare to find a poverty-stricken Jew, even in very poor countries. When they immigrate, a few from the family go first, get established, and then bring the next ones over and help them get established and so on. They may not be rich, but they are not in need and rarely dependent on anyone outside of the family. This is not just savvy business; it's God's principles of family responsibility being lived out.

In today's independent world we focus on self-reliance. That is not entirely bad, but in scripture God clearly balances independence with family and community responsibility. The view of family today is contributing to the new poor and to economic ruin for the community and the individual.

Family: First Line Of Defense – Justice

Deuteronomy 21:15-21 can be disturbing if we are reading it for application and not principle:

> 15 If a man has two wives, and he loves one but not the other, and both bear him sons but the firstborn is the son of the wife he does not love,
> 16 when he wills his property to his sons, he must not give the rights of the firstborn to the son of the wife he loves in preference to his actual firstborn, the son of the wife he does not love.
> 17 He must acknowledge the son of his unloved wife as the firstborn by giving him a double share of all he has. That son is the first sign of his father's strength. The right of the firstborn belongs to him.
> 18 If a man has a stubborn and rebellious son who does not obey his father and mother and will not listen to them when they discipline him,
> 19 his father and mother shall take hold of him and bring him to the elders at the gate of his town.
> 20 They shall say to the elders, "This son of ours is stubborn and rebellious. He will not obey us. He is a profligate and a drunkard."

21 Then all the men of his town shall stone him to death. You must purge the evil from among you. All Israel will hear of it and be afraid.

This passage is not a teaching *for* polygamy or capital punishment of teenagers. At the time Moses is writing these passages the tribes are polygamous and violent. The guideline "an eye for and eye and tooth for a tooth" is already an attempt to curtail their vengeful justice system in which they take "a life for a slap."[12] God has never been oblivious to the realities of the peoples He is discipling and God is not unrealistic. Discipleship takes time and a step in the right direction is a good step. Monogamy is clearly God's highest in an overview of scripture, but they are polygamous at this time in history and, within that less than desirable state of affairs, there must still be justice. The overwhelming importance of this passage and similar laws is that: "family members have rights, whether men, women or children" and that "family members have a responsibility to honor those rights and to carry out those responsibilities."

No record in scripture tells of a rebellious teenager being stoned. And I don't think that is surprising. The overwhelming message of this passage is parental responsibility. Parents must invest the time and be responsible to discipline. If that is not effective, they have to bring the child to the leaders. It is the community's responsibility to weigh whether the parents have done all that is possible and if the child is truly incorrigible. Another passage tells us that the parents have to lead in applying the punishment. The principle is not that "rebellious teenagers are to be stoned;" the principle God is putting forward here is that **"parents *are* responsible for the actions of their children."**

In the book of Esther, we see a wonderful example of family responsibilities being carried out. Esther is an orphan and a refugee. Her cousin, Mordecai, raises her as his daughter. He is instrumental in her becoming Queen of Babylon. Mordecai modeled a passion for justice not only in his family but also in his community. When the pagan king, who holds the Jews in exile by force, is in danger of assassination, it is Mordecai who warns of the plot and saves the king's life.[13] Then Mordecai calls upon Esther to use her position as queen to save the Jewish people from a plot

---

12. *Genesis 4:23 -24*
13. *Esther 2:19*

of genocide hatched by Haman, another political leader. Mordecai lived by the rule of "loving your neighbor as yourself" and modeled it in caring for his family, his host country, and, finally, for his own people. He understood that justice included "loving your neighbor." His simple modeling of that to a family member, Esther, resulted in the saving of a nation.

Jesus says the whole of the law can be summed up by this sentence: "Love God and love your neighbor as yourself." James calls this the royal law[14] and goes on to say that showing favoritism in applying this law is sin. What happens when children observe discrimination in their own home? Parents speak of justice for strangers, but treat each other unjustly. A pastor preaches love on Sunday, but beats his wife. We talk of God loving the lost, but show intolerance for different ethnic groups or "types" of sinners. We constantly criticize our government, but don't even vote. How can we raise children to believe and model justice if justice is not modeled in the home? How can we hope to influence our communities if we do not model community concern and action at home? The answer? We can't. The family is God's first line of defence for individual and community justice.

Family: First Line Of Defense – Love

God summarizes the whole of His thinking about life in one word: love. God's definition of love means the presence of justice, provision, integrity, truth. The authority behind government as God created it to function is the people. The authority of science is the unchangeable, God-created laws of nature. The authority of the church is its right handling of the Word of God. Authority is expressed in the family domain through love – love that is defined by the way Christ loved the church.

The younger leaders I work with in ministry have a hard time with the fact that I still teach structure in the family. I am open and listening, but until I see their view in the Word I have to withhold changing my thinking. As I look at the whole of the Bible, I see structure in every institution God has created. It seems to me that He has designed us to live that way and the universe to function that way. I see family structure in scripture. The parents have authority over the children until they leave home, and the husband over the wife. I know some hate

---

14. James 2:8

to see those words; we have a knee jerk reaction because the concept has been abused and made to mean things God could never condone. Many in history have abused scripture in order to make themselves more powerful. But, what does God mean by these texts?

Ephesians 5:22-6:4

22 Wives, submit to your husbands as to the Lord.

23 For the husband is the head of the wife as Christ is the head of the church, his body, of which he is the Savior.

24 Now as the church submits to Christ, so also wives should submit to their husbands in everything.

25 Husbands, love your wives, just as Christ loved the church and gave himself up for her

26 to make her holy, cleansing her by the washing with water through the word,

27 and to present her to himself as a radiant church, without stain or wrinkle or any other blemish, but holy and blameless.

28 In this same way, husbands ought to love their wives as their own bodies. He who loves his wife loves himself.

29 After all, no one ever hated his own body, but he feeds and cares for it, just as Christ does the church –

30 for we are members of his body.

31 "For this reason a man will leave his father and mother and be united to his wife, and the two will become one flesh."

32 This is a profound mystery – but I am talking about Christ and the church.

33 However, each one of you also must love his wife as he loves himself, and the wife must respect her husband.

1 Children, obey your parents in the Lord, for this is right.

2 "Honor your father and mother" – which is the first commandment with a promise –

3 "that it may go well with you and that you may enjoy long life on the earth."

4 Fathers, do not exasperate your children; instead, bring them up in the training and instruction of the Lord.

If we move this discussion of structure and authority in the family away from "who takes out the garbage" and "who does the laundry" and move it to who is responsible and when are they responsible, then I think God's view becomes clearer. For instance, if a spouse is unconscious in the hospital and needs surgery, who should be able to give consent? If a family member borrows money and fails to pay, who should be responsible? If a parent dies in an accident, who should get the children? Who should take financial responsibility for children until they are old enough to take care of themselves? Governments have to make laws to guide decisions like those that communities make every day and our "world – view" of family will determine those decisions. The emphasis of God's word is clear: A great deal of responsibility belongs in the family domain.

The Authority Of Family Is Love

So there is structure and authority in the family. Now, how is that authority to be carried out? When is the authority of family being abused and to be forfeited? When should a child be taken from a home? When must a spouse flee a marriage? When should the government take authority away from parents? How do we determine the difference between parental discipline and abuse of a child? Difficult questions! Really, the essence of these questions is, "When does family have authority and when does the community or the government step in?"

How do we define love? The Word says love is demonstrated in the way Jesus works with the church and the way a person takes care of his or her own body. Love says, "*You* are as important to *me* as *me*." In fact, this kind of love says, "You are more important to me than me." Because Christ gave up His life and his right to authority in order to serve the church. He gave up his body and life that we might have life.

Wow! This is radical stuff. Husbands, this means that, if you are to have authority with your wives, you must be "chief lover." Your authority in your home is based on the quality of your love! Parents, in order to have authority over your children you will need to love them. The less faithful your love, the less authority you will have with them. In fact, if you act in a way that is actually destructive to your spouse or children, you have no authority and they can and *should* be taken from you.

Should a spouse or child endure life-threatening abuse because God gives authority to that family structure? Absolutely not. God *never* gives all authority over all things at all times to anyone! He is the only one He would trust with that kind of authority and He even limits Himself. In creating you and me in His image, He limited His control over our lives by giving us free will. That freedom has rights and responsibilities for each of us, but when anyone tries to remove that freedom entirely in the name of any authority it is called tyranny.

To understand what Paul means when he teaches us to submit to the authority of government, look at how he lived that submission out. When the Roman government ordered him to stop preaching he disobeyed their authority and willingly went to prison for it. There was a higher law over his faith and actions: God Himself. When the government exercised authority not given to it by the people or by God, Paul entered into civil disobedience. This subject is a book within itself, but my point here is that no one, including family, has all authority over anyone; to honor, submit, and obey in scripture does not always mean doing what you are told. This concept is probably most abused in the arena of family.

Destructive Myths Floating Around Christian Families

Men are over women:

Sorry, no such principle in scripture. In fact, Barak lost his military honors for not following the orders of his Commandress in Chief, Deborah. There is no overall mandate in scripture of men in authority over women. There is a structure to family and the authority for that structure is love.

We will only want sex with one lifetime partner:

Sorry again! The Bible seems to assume that we will have sex with just about anyone or anything unless we are taught differently. In the Old Testament God teaches sexual conduct in great detail and in the New Testament Jesus teaches that all temptations are common and, furthermore, that He experienced them all!

Love means never having to say I'm sorry:

No! Love means the presence of justice, provision, protection, and harmony. "Love is patient, love is kind. It does not envy, it does not boast, it is not proud. It is not rude, it is not self-seeking, it is not easily angered, it keeps no record of wrongs. Love does not delight in evil but rejoices with the truth. It always protects, always trusts, always hopes, always perseveres." 1 Corinthians 13:4-7

I need sex to be happy and fulfilled:

If that were true, surely we would be one of the happiest and most fulfilled generations in history. No, scripture does say we need intimacy in relationships to be happy and fulfilled, but we can have that with or without sex. There is nothing more lonely than sex without intimacy and nothing more fulfilling than intimacy with or without sex. We must marry for the right reasons or we will continue to have marriages that fail.

Staying together is the key:

Staying married is less financially damaging and often better for everyone, especially the children. But when we move the discussion to "why marry in the first place" and God's purpose for marriage, we can work on staying together for the right reason. Until then, our cures are all bandages on a hemorrhage.

A good marriage will always feel good:

Wrong! In God's design, a good marriage will rub against both spouses' rough edges until you are smoothed more into the image of Christ. Part of the purpose of marriage is to help deliver us from ourselves by bringing us face to face with ourselves in a loving environment.

STUDY HELP:

Themes to consider when studying and coloring the subject of family in scripture: *wives, husbands, sons, daughters, children, widows, orphans, principles and ethics of relationships, sexual conduct.*

The domain of family reveals: **The Father**
The primary attribute of God revealed in the family: **Love/Nurture**
God governs this domain through: **The laws of love**
The color I used: **Orange**

WORKING VOCATIONAL MISSION STATEMENT:

The purpose of family is to provide a safe, nurturing environment for growth, values, and development of the next generation. It is the smallest building block of human society. **Great issues include:** Love, discipline, modeling God's thinking, preparation for vocation of the children and the husband's love setting the tone of the home.

A NOTE TO ALL BELIEVERS:

We all live in families and our first witness is how we live there. We can accomplish nothing greater in our community or in nations than what we accomplish in the microcosm of our own home and family. We will reproduce who we are, and who we are is most revealed in our home where we are known on a daily basis. This is not a trap; this is God's design. Our close relationships give us a mirror in which to see how much we are reflecting His glory. In our family we see what God wants to work on in our lives to make us more loving, more like Himself. This is an ongoing lifelong process of growth. Each stage of life gives us opportunity to grow in new areas. He is there to help us. Marriage, children, adolescence, empty nest, death, middle age, grandchildren, old age, illness all give us opportunity to grow with each other in the family. This is called living and with Christ it is called abundant living, being made more like Him on a daily basis. Family is a sacred covenant meant to produce God-likeness in us all. When you grow here you will take more of Jesus into everything you do and you will reproduce His likeness.

A NOTE TO FAMILY PROFESSIONALS:

Whether you are a family counselor, family lawyer, social worker, or any other family-oriented professional, yours is one of the most important arenas in society. If the family is healthy, we will have healthy communities and, then, healthy nations. It is so important that you see your work and the role of family from God's perspective. We must touch family structures very lightly and invade only in the direst of circumstances. However, we must not allow abusive injustice to rule in any family. When and how to step into a family unit to save the individual is a vital and delicate balance. Only God's perspective and His wisdom can help us in individual cases and in making policies, guidelines and laws that bridle our profession's authority so that it does not destroy the very institution it is there to protect. You have a wonderful and sacred call; fulfill it in the wisdom and power of His Spirit.

CHAPTER 11
Education

"Fix these words of mine in your hearts and minds; tie them as symbols on your hands and bind them on your foreheads. Teach them to your children, talking about them when you sit at home and when you walk along the road, when you lie down and when you get up. Write them on the door frames of your houses and on your gates, so that our days and the days of your children may be many in the land that the Lord swore to give your forefathers, as many as the days that the heavens are above the earth."

Deuteronomy 11:18-21

"Love the Lord your God with all your heart and with all your soul and with all your strength and with all your mind"

Luke 10:27

Education, like communication and the arts, is difficult to isolate and study apart from other areas in scripture. Everything in scripture is about learning. The Bible is a book inspired by God for our education and understanding of His ways. So, again, with this chapter we do not have one scripture that serves as an example, but will look at a scriptural overview of the subject. It is clear that God is a God of knowledge. He can be known. He wants to be known and He wants us to know Him in all that He has made. You could say that inquiring minds are godly minds and one of the primary marks of discipleship is expressed in questions – the desire to learn and know.

We *Can* Know

Epistemology is a big word meaning the "science of knowing." All philosophies and religions ask, "Can we know?" and, if so, "How can we know?" God's Word says, "Yes, we *can* know!" And we will know through a combined process of discovery and revelation. The basis of modern science – that the material world is real, measurable, and discoverable – is a biblical concept. The Islamic world can copy technology, but has a very hard time creating and maintaining it because they believe there are no fixed laws by which God governs the material world. There is only the will of Allah. Hinduism and Buddhism teach, basically, that the material world we live in is not real and not important. Many Christian doctrines get dangerously close to this split concept today. But the Bible teaches that truth is discoverable and knowable and that, when applied, consistently results in the same consequences. God knows all truth and all truth, in any and every domain of life, reveals God. Mystery in scripture is a result of the difference between what we know and what God knows, not what is knowable. In His Word, God originates and encourages wisdom, knowledge, and education.

Education Reveals The Attribute Of Wisdom

For the Hebrew mind discipled by the teaching of Moses the concept of knowing included *application*. This is far from most worldviews today. Most educational systems are based on the concept that you can *know* by retaining information about a subject without needing to apply it. As a result, the working world acknowledges that university graduates can do nothing when they first come to work. They have to be taught *how* on the job. This greatly concerns educational professionals worldwide and has become a subject of debate and study. This same idea – that data is knowledge – has led to a generation of Christians who say they know God but still don't know how to obey Him. Many have the concept that you can *know* the writer of scripture without applying any of His principles, that you can be saved but not demonstrate any fruit of that conversion in your daily life, or, as some say, "believe like God and act like the devil." None of these are biblical assumptions.

From Genesis through the book of Revelation, God reinforces the concept that knowledge is demonstrated in action, faith in works, learning in growth, wisdom in love. There is no scriptural basis for a "blind leap of faith." Existentialism says you cannot *know,* you can only *experience.* Jesus refused to leap off the temple at Satan's temptation. Jesus understood that you could know the will of God without taking the leap. The "experience" of leaping was not the only way to know. For God, wisdom is not just choosing right, but understanding why it is right. God's goal is not, finally, obedience but agreement. As parents we understand that in the beginning we must just say, "No," to a child who is about to put his little hand on a hot burner. We try to convey that it is hot and he will be burned, but when he is small, we are satisfied if he just doesn't touch it. As he matures we are looking for him to become aware of what we mean by *hot* and, hopefully without permanent damage, begin to agree that burning flesh is a bad and painful thing. Finally, we want him not to touch the burner because he agrees that it would not be a good thing to do.

If we are growing in God, we'll need to ask about fewer and fewer things because we've learned God's thinking on those subject. This does not mean that we no longer are inquiring of God. It means we no longer ask God the same question because we come to know and agree with His answers and reasoning. We will learn and ask God about things that are new for us because we do not yet have God's mindset on them.

The Old and New Testaments are full of admonitions to add to the experience of knowing God personally, to gain information about God revealed in creation, history, and the written word. Paul writes of "renewing our minds"[1] and "taking every thought captive and making it conform to the *mind* of Christ."[2] In 1 Colossians 14:15 he encourages the church to pray with their minds, with understanding, as well as in tongues. In Acts the people of God were gathered in "one heart *and one mind.*"[3] Paul warns of a "sinful mind" in Romans 8:6 and admonishes the Romans to have a "mind controlled by the Spirit." The entirety of Proverbs celebrates the blessings of wisdom applied to our lives and encourages the

1. *Romans 12:2*
2. *Corinthians 10:5*
3. *Acts 4:32*

life-long pursuit of her. Over and over again in the books of Moses the Israelites are admonished to study and learn the ways of God revealed in the Torah and to apply them to their lives. Jesus had mastered these principles by the time he was twelve and astounded the priests with His wisdom.[4] One difference between Jesus and the Pharisees was that they quoted the Law, but He explained it. He understood it. He could apply it to daily life. Jesus calls His disciples to, "Ask, seek, knock..." to inquire and learn of Him and His Father. All of the prophets admonished Israel to turn back to the principles laid down by God through Moses and to see the blessing of God return.

Repentance Means Changed Thinking

The New Testament word *repent* is often taught to mean *change direction*. The actual translation of the word from the Greek would be *change thinking*. In other words, the key to changed behavior is changed thought, not the other way around. When we focus on actions, we become obsessed with the appearance rather than the substance of our lives. We *look* good but we are unchanged on the inside. God's concern is not so much with the external, but who we are internally. God desires to win us to His view of reality and truth so that we are like Him because we see reality as He sees it.

In chapter 10 of 2 Corinthians Paul argues that our warfare is a warfare, in part, of the mind. "For though we live in the world, we do not wage war as the world does. The weapons we fight with are not the weapons of the world. On the contrary, they have divine power to demolish strongholds. We demolish arguments and every pretension that sets itself up against the knowledge of God, and we take captive every thought to make it obedient to Christ."[5] Our warfare with this world is the warfare of ideas and reality. If we are to stand and be an influence, we must not only act as Jesus would act, we must think as Jesus thinks.

---

4. *Luke 2:46-47*
5. *Corinthians 10:3-5*

Education And The Family

In an "Economist" article in the late 90's, researchers wrote of discovering that successful learning in the classroom had little to do with how much money or time was spent on the subject. They found that less learning could take place when more time and money had been spent and vice versa. One determining factor for success or failure was the method of teaching. Parental support was another factor that educators worldwide agree is important. If parents are involved in the child's education the child will learn more. Scripture overwhelmingly agrees with this discovery; the authority and responsibility of parents in teaching their children is abundantly clear.

In the future, when your son asks you, "what is the meaning of the stipulations, decrees and laws the Lord our God has commanded you?" tell him:

Deuteronomy 6:20-25

We were slaves of Pharaoh in Egypt, but the Lord brought us out of Egypt with a mighty hand. Before our eyes the Lord sent miraculous signs and wonders – great and terrible – upon Egypt and Pharaoh and his whole household. But he brought us out from there to bring us in and give us the land that he promised on oath to our forefathers. The Lord commanded us to obey all these decrees and to fear the Lord our God, so that we might always prosper and be kept alive, as is the case today. And if we are careful to obey all this law before the Lord our God, as he has commanded us, that will be our righteousness.

Deuteronomy 11:19-21

Teach them to your children, talking about them when you sit at home and when your walk along the road, when you lie down and when you get up. Write them on the door frames of your houses and on your gates, so that your days and the days of your children may be many in the land that the Lord swore to give your forefathers, as many as the days that the heavens are above the earth.

Children Absorb Their World View

As we discussed in the chapter on Family, in those formative years from birth to four, when children absorb the view of reality around them, the parents' perspective is the critical factor. The child *will* take in the values and beliefs that are modeled in the home, whether they are intentionally taught by the parents or not. The child will believe the reality parents convey and will copy it. They have no choice at this stage of growth because they are exposed to no other reality. Parents will imprint their actual, not necessarily desired, value system on the child. For this reason God emphasizes, over and over again, the importance of parents teaching their children God's view of life in the everyday activities of eating, walking and working together.

I am not proposing that scripture indicates all parents should home school. That is just one method of education and the Bible does not put forth a single model. However, the influence of parents in the child's life is emphasized in the Word. Based on their parents' view, children will go to school believing they are smart enough, or too stupid, to learn. They will enter school believing learning is important and exciting, or boring and a waste of time, based on their parents' view. When they come home, the importance of homework will be reinforced, or devalued; home will be a place that promotes learning or a place that disrupts it. From home they will take the idea that something can be learned from everyone and that everyone's ideas need to be evaluated or, perhaps, they will take the belief that there is nothing to learn from anyone. Before they ever go to school, children will believe in a God who reveals truth, or that there is no truth.

Have your ever wondered why God spends so much time on the early life of Daniel and his training in Babylon? Daniel and his three friends are captive aliens in Babylon, taken from their families as adolescents into the palace and service of the King. They attend Babylon University where they study witchcraft, divination, and other sordid subjects, and they are at the top of their class. They are surrounded by a pagan, idolatrous culture, yet none of them absorbs any of it. How do we explain this in a world where Christians and non-Christians alike are declaring television, movies, music, advertising, and schools to be the formative influences on young people's minds? How did Daniel and the others stand in this Babylonian environment? The answer is simple and profoundly emphasized in scripture: they took their values with them. They continued to weigh the values around them in captivity with what they had been taught and, more importantly, modeled in their homes. Scripture indicates that if children are the victims of the world around them, there can only be one explanation. They are not being given the tools at home to evaluate the messages coming at them from the world, and they have not been given the confidence that they, with God's help, can know and discern truth.

Education And Government

For several decades Christians in my country have been very vocal about the damage to our public school system caused by removal of prayer from schools. I do not want to argue for the absence of prayer, but I do want to discuss the thinking behind this argument. First of all, from God's perspective you cannot outlaw prayer; you can only outlaw prayer meetings and praying out loud. God has given no authority to government to rule over our hearts and minds. We can think and believe what we like. The institution of government can only attempt to control our outward actions. For decades we have traced the decline of our schools and education in the U.S.A. to a law banning prayer when law cannot ban prayer unless we agree to it. The law is unjust, but is it catastrophic?

On the other hand, something else took place in the U.S. that perhaps had far greater implications. The authority of education began to move consistently from parent- and teacher-based local organizations towards a national association for education. This shift in authority from family to government was far more strategic and dangerous than outlawing prayer meetings. God gave no authority to governments over our children. God gave that authority to parents. Governments are created by God to deal with the masses. By design, that is their function. Education, by its nature, is an individual process. Like social issues of poverty and drugs, if you ask the government to deal with it, you will have the most expensive and least effective programs. The government will design a program that attempts to deal with everyone in the same way...much like a prison system. But social problems, drugs, and education are individual problems that can only be solved effectively by addressing the individual. God designed the family to deal with individuals. Parents can delegate their authority to a public school system, but if they abdicate their support or if their role is ignored or even denied by the institution, those schools have very little legitimate authority over the children.

The same is true when parents abdicate responsibility for their child's education to a Christian school. God does not give the church the responsibility to train children. He gives that responsibility to parents.

Education And The Laws Of Human Nature

In education and in communication it is important to look at how God has created human nature to work. Today's media culture emphasizes the power of persuasion to the point that we begin to think of ourselves more as recorders, taking every message in and conforming to it. When a crisis hits, we blame the impact of the media, or schools, or postmodernism, and the way youth think today. We talk about "secular" education as though it is a power in and of itself.

This is not the view of man conveyed in scripture. In the Bible, the human race is given great authority, the authority to accept or reject the influences around them. Nothing in God's Word indicates that it is easy to make our fellowman do what we want. Far from it. Scripture emphasizes man's ability to discern, and accept or reject, influences around him. In the next chapter on communication we will discuss brainwashing, subliminal communication and the "recordable man" theories. But for the sake of our discussion on education, let me summarize by saying that, once we move on from those very formative first years, we learn what we want to learn. We are far more like filters than sponges. This is so profoundly true that communists in the former Soviet Union can drum doctrine into school children for seven decades and yet no more than twenty percent of them believe in communism. Generations of black children in South Africa were taught that they are to have no role in the political life of their nation, yet almost none of them believe it. Maori and European children in New Zealand attend the same schools and come out with incredibly different world-views.

Educators I've talked to all over the world agree that the two most important keys to learning are the parents' attitude and involvement, and the motivation of the child. The biblical view is that every child is gifted, every child can learn, every child has value, and every child has the right to reach its full potential. But it also emphasizes that we are created by God to be free and we make choices whether to hear (learn) or not. The greatest influence on those choices will be the first few years in our home environment.

Why do I emphasize this? Because we have to recognize what an education system can and cannot do. We have to realize the importance of parenting. We have to give schools their proper place in God's scheme of things, but not expect them to work miracles or work in isolation. And, we have to put our faith for the future in more than education.

STUDY HELP:

Themes to consider when studying and coloring the subject of education in scripture: *teaching, learning, remembering, mind, thought, reason, nurture, wisdom and family.*

The domain of education reveals: **The Great Teacher-Rabbi**
The primary attribute of God revealed in education: **Wisdom**
God governs this domain through: **The laws of human nature**
The color I used: **Brown**

WORKING VOCATIONAL MISSION STATEMENT:

To provide for the development of the God-given gifts in every child for the service of their fellow man and society, believing every child is gifted by God and has the right for those gifts to be developed to their highest potential. **Great issues include:** Value-based integrated process with family involvement and support.

A NOTE TO ALL BELIEVERS:

Do you love learning? God does! Are you interested in everything? God is! If we are to model Jesus to those around us, part of that modeling will be His passion to know His Father in every area of life. One of the most tragic effects of the split gospel is the loss of interest in most of life. Often it seems that the only thing a believer can talk about is church, prayer, heaven, and hell. Not that those are not important. They are! But, were Jesus here, He would be ecstatic to be in the first generation to actually see through the Hubble telescope a star being born, or dying. His Father created that and He would worship Him in all that the heavens are still teaching us. He would stand in awe at the way His Father created the DNA of the human species. He would ponder the fact that every cell can reproduce every other human cell and what that says about the nature and character of God. Jesus would love the idea of going to other planets and discovering more of what the Father has made. He would be reading, listening, eager about what is going on in His Father's cosmos and He would be excited about what we are learning and how God wants to use that insight.

God has made us with the capacity to learn – or to refuse to learn, to know – or to refuse to know. From Genesis to Revelation God portrays Himself as the Lord of knowledge, revealed in all the truths of the universe. Choose to think like God! Choose to be interested. Model Jesus' love of learning and you will make those around you hungry for more.

Children love learning unless they are taught to be afraid of it. All it takes to learn is willingness to admit you don't know. That is the humility of a child. Children naturally ask questions. They have to be taught to feel foolish about the eagerness to know things. God loves questions and calls us to "ask, seek, knock"...and become like children again.

A NOTE TO EDUCATIONAL PROFESSIONALS:

Wherever I speak on this subject educational professionals ask me what they can do to influence their education system. The first thing I tell them is to study God's word until they believe they see learning from

God's perspective. Zeal without wisdom is not good. Secondly, whatever their position, they can seek more parental involvement. As a teacher, they can communicate with and seek communication from their students' parents. They can organize parental dialogue about the school system and their classroom. In many countries parents can be invited to volunteer and add to the curriculum and classroom management. How we do it is not as important as what we believe is essential. The critical thing is that we understand God's principles. The applications will be dynamic to our community's specific situation.

I love the story Bruce Olsen conveys of his experiences with the Motilone Indians in South America.[6] This tribe was Stone Age and almost entirely isolated from the outside world when Bruce went to live with them. An amazing move of God took place among these people and the entire tribe was converted to Christ. As they grew in God and began to understand more of the importance of scripture, they believed they needed to tackle the issue of education and learning to read. Rather than imposing a system on the Indians, Bruce Olson asked how they wanted to go about the process of education. The tribe decided that the elders needed to learn to read first so that they could then teach the children, otherwise the fiber of authority in the tribe would be destroyed. If the elders learned first, the importance of learning would be enhanced and they would be able to model for the children the value of learning to read. What a great application.

As administrator and school board members we should be seeking influence and policy that brings back parental involvement and authority in our school system. This is not to say that government does not have a role in organizing and overseeing an educational system. It is to say the system must be as parent- and local-based in its authority as possible. As a local principal you can create a voice for parents whether in a formal or informal way. You can create a communication strategy that helps them feel informed and involved and you can help your classroom teachers do the same. I do not mean to imply that getting parents involved is an easy task. Apathy abounds. However, the more the parents are involved, the healthier the school system will be.

---

6. Olsen, Bruce, "Bruchko", YWAM Publishing, May 2005

CHAPTER 12
Communication

"And God said, 'Let there be light,' and there was light."

Genesis 1:3

"Do you have eyes but fail to see, and ears but fail to hear?"

Mark 8:18

"Instead, I have called you friends, for everything that I learned from my father I have made known to you."

John 15:15

God Is Communication

Of all the domains, communication is the most difficult to isolate and study. The entire Bible is made up of books, poems, and letters, which God intended, along with everything else He made, to communicate Himself. He is the Word. The visible world reveals His invisible attributes. Man is made in His image. The Holy Spirit leads us into all truth and Jesus reveals the Father. Everything God does is communication and everything you and I do communicates. We are communicators made in the image of a communicating God. One great difference between biblical thought and all other worldviews and religions is that scripture records God communicating with man while others are attempting to find God. Again, we have no single text for this domain because the entire Bible is communication, but we will look at an overview of the subject.

God compares Himself to words. He calls Himself the *Living Word* and says that words have power if we give them power. As much as any other arena, the domain of communication reveals the sovereign will of God's human creation and our individual ability to choose to listen, see, believe, and say what we like. God will not overrule that sovereignty of the individual, even for His own message. We have the power, we have the right, to accept or reject anyone's ideas, concepts, or words. Our job as Christians is not to overpower others with our view of the world, but to persuasively communicate our message – to give others a choice so that, by the grace of God, "we might win some."

We Are Sovereign

God is sovereign and, created in His image, we are sovereign. What are we sovereign over? We are sovereign over ourselves. We should not sin, but we can sin. God does not desire to be separated from us, but we can choose to separate from Him. We do not have to spend eternity in heaven; we can accept or reject the truth when it is presented to us. When we study communication and the domain of the individual we see the power of sovereignty and just how wonderfully, and terrifyingly, we are made.

Research reveals that we are literally able to see and hear what we want to see and hear. We filter out messages that we reject or that make us uncomfortable. For example family members of alcoholics literally cannot see the pattern of abuse because it is too painful. Whole people groups can be virtually invisible within a culture, such as women in Afghanistan or Indians in America. I see this every year in the productions of our communications students' videos. Whether Asian, black, islander or white, they fill their pieces with their own kind. No matter what the dominant race on location, they film those who are like them because that is whom *they* see.

This difference of perspective is so predictable in human society, that if two or three witnesses in court testify that they have seen exactly the same things, the testimony is thrown out. It is assumed by the court that they have collaborated on their testimony. We have such a powerful sovereign will that we are literally able to rule over the messages we are willing to receive and reject.

Today's World View

Today, the view amongst most non-Christians and Christians alike is the opposite of what God stresses in His Word. We claim that culture, family, individuals are being destroyed by television, movies, music, and mass media. But God says in His Word that He has placed authority with the individual; he has given His human creation the power to choose.

If communication media were powerful in and of themselves, evangelism of the world would be simple and cheap; we could just broadcast God's Word from every street corner in the world. The power of the media would overwhelm people and they would be converted. Or we could use television or radio. But as soon as converts were exposed to a different message they would be unconverted. If they watched Christian T.V., they would convert, but if they switched the channel and watched an atheist program they would unconvert. Of course, this is ridiculous and I am being facetious, but that is a fair conclusion to this exaggerated sense of media power. The media are not powerful in and of themselves. They are an influence that we, the audience, choose to empower or not. God clearly conveys in His word that power on earth rests with the individual. Why? Because that is the way God made us.

Does that mean content doesn't matter? No, not at all. There is good content and bad content, good quality and poor quality. But at the end of the day, people have watched and listened to what they want to be influenced by. The popularity of a given message is a reflection of the audience, not the power of the message itself. The power belongs to the individual and when we embrace this as the way God created us to function, we embrace our role as communicators who offer people a choice.

Jesus Did Not Silence Anyone

If we are to think like God, we must be more concerned with what is *not* being conveyed through the media than what is. We get so busy trying to silence those who disagree with us that we fail to notice that the truth is not being conveyed. We worry that the Internet is proliferating pornography and forget the printing press did the same thing. The Guttenberg press that helped create a revolution in printing the Bible also created a revolution of smut. Technology is neutral. It multiplies the message, good or bad. So for what "good" are we to use the Internet? What alternative are we giving those who are surfing the web? The problem with the media since the invention of the television is what is missing rather than what is there. Are there choices? Can the truth be found? That is our responsibility as God's people. We can see this in the life of Jesus.

If you study the New Testament carefully, you will find no documentation of Jesus silencing anyone...except demons, and they were all speaking the truth.[1] Jesus made no attempt to stifle the voice of the Romans, the Greeks, the Zealots, the Pharisees, or any of the hundreds of messages flooding His region of the world that He did not agree with. All were given free reign to continue disseminating any message they believed in. Jesus did, on the other hand, safeguard His right to continue freely bringing His message until He knew it was time for his arrest.

The absence of righteousness and truth in others' messages was not a concern to Him. He focused on the freedom to bring His message into that open forum. God was giving people a choice, not demanding control of what they were hearing. Truth, in a free forum, speaks for itself. God is not interested in hiding evil. God is interested in us comparing light to darkness and making a choice between the two. Truth in the midst of a free forum is self-evident. The absence of righteousness means people have no choice. Rather than focusing on what is in the public forum, our concern as the people of God should be what is missing. Rather than spending all our energy on silencing those we disagree with, we should spend time making our message available. Scripture indicates that the light actually has more impact in darkness.

Developed Vs. Undeveloped

These principles of communication, applied to communities and nations, produce interesting evidence. Not *one* developed country today is without a free press. Perhaps more importantly, not one undeveloped country *has* a free press. It would seem that the freedom of expression of ideas is tied directly to people feeling responsible for their societies. It is

---

1. *Mark 3:11*

true, with a free press, lies can be told and the freedom abused, but with a free press, the truth can be told and people can make a choice.

Christians who believed in the right to communicate began the first newspaper in the United States. The masthead of that paper read, "To Cure The Spirit Of Lying." The only thing needed to bring salt and light to a free nation with a free communication system is someone willing to tell the truth. If we want to secure the right to a free forum for our own message, we must defend others' right to speak.

Words have power, but they are not the power of control; they are the power of influence. God does not seek to take control of us; He seeks to offer choices and, by seeing the worth of His truth, win us to Himself. He has made us sovereign over our own mind and soul, over our destiny. His desire is that we use our eyes to see the difference between deception and reality, our ears to hear the difference between lies and truth. God does not want to hide evil, He wants us to be able to see it for what it is and make a choice. We have embraced non-biblical thinking when we make the message more powerful than the person.

The Medium Is Not The Message

Christians were ecstatic when Guttenberg first invented movable type. Printing could now put inexpensive Bibles in the hands of believers. The use of this technological innovation by the church was such a revolution that Christian publishing still outnumbers all other uses in the industry. As newspapers evolved, Christians were in the forefront. The Salvation Army produced the first feature-length movie. Christian communicators have such passion for the use of radio that Christians today own more radio licenses worldwide than any other single group.

With the emergence of television, computers, and the Internet, however, the Christian thinking on media changed dramatically. Rather than seeing new technology as an opportunity for making the truth known in new ways, it was seen as a threat and, perhaps, evil in and of itself because of its potential to carry destructive messages. This shift in the view of communication has resulted in an absence of any significant contribution to these media. The early leaders in the film industry were self-governing and religious leaders were automatically included in review boards. The Christian leaders pulled out of this "secular" arena, rather than being asked to leave by the film industry. As God gives us the greatest communication technologies in the history of man, there is little vision or passion for the use of these new media.

Of course, this view of technology is not biblical. All scientific discovery is morally neutral. Only the use of it could be classified as good or evil. If we do not repent of our wrong thinking in this area, the "age of communication" may be known in history as the darkest age of all.

The Importance Of Words

Throughout the Old Testament and into the New the importance of our words is dramatically emphasized. Whether in relationship to keeping promises and vows, testimony and bearing witness, treaties or agreements with other nations, or our accountability before God for every word, the importance is weighty. The Jewish community still understands these communication principles and is committed to the communication industry, making their story known, and retaining respect for the verbal contract.

There could be no more dramatic difference between the Jews and their Arab cousins than this view of words. We are flabbergasted as we watch leaders from another region of the world on television swear that there is no invading army, even as tanks roll in behind him. At first glance, we think that is just arrogance or stupidity, but it is far more important than that. Their ability to say something completely unrelated to apparent facts is tied to two beliefs: one, there are no objective facts – *truth* is whatever God wants to be true; and, two, words mean nothing. In a world-view where God is the *only* reality, where there are no checks and balances to that reality, words mean little because no reality can be communicated. We mean nothing and our words mean nothing. This is very close to the post-modern idea of "reality is anything I believe it to be."

It is impossible to overstate the Judaic/Christian influence of reality and truth of communication on the development of justice, science, economics, and general quality of life in the West. Our entire concept of contracts, testimony, agreements, and relationships are built on the importance and the reality of words. Much of our frustration in dealing with the East, the Middle East and beyond is that we fail to realize this view of communication has not been part of the building blocks of these cultures. Part of "teaching the nations" is laying a biblical foundation of communication.

STUDY HELP:

Themes to consider when studying and coloring the subject of communication in scripture: *the use of the book, poetry, historical, speeches, scribes, messengers, the tongue, words, scrolls, tablets, monuments, writing, signs, storytelling.*

The domain of communication reveals: **The Living Word**
The primary attribute of God revealed in communication: **Sovereignty**
God governs this domain through: **The laws of human nature**
The color I used: **Red**

WORKING VOCATIONAL MISSION STATEMENT:

To provide truthful, objective information of importance to the community-at-large so that citizens can make informed decisions.

A NOTE TO ALL BELIEVERS:

I always get quite an audience reaction with this teaching on communication. Parents argue that they don't want their children exposed to everything that is out there; others ask if I am defending everything that is on T.V. and in movies. I get questions about record-burning and library standards for the community. Much of this is put forth with a great deal of emotion.

As parents or responsible adults caring for young children, we have to set a standard for what is good and what we approve of, and what is "premature" for a child to be exposed to. We have the right and the responsibility to do this. However, we must also prepare the child for young adulthood where he will no longer be protected by others and may be exposed, in a fallen world, to almost anything. If the result of our discipleship is confidence and discernment in the young adult then, like Daniel's parents, we have done a good job. If the result in the young adult is fear and the need to live an insular life then we have produced a cripple and a Christian who must live in a cave. Rather than knowing how to be in the world and not of it, we have produced a religious hermit who cannot be in the world at all. We clearly cannot be salt and light in hiding.

What this means, then, is that we must teach our charges the standards to use in discerning the communication that will come across their path. We must teach them to interpret the message, discern the thinking behind it. What is biblical and what is not? There is danger in how truth is communicated as well. Would we be able to discern that it was demons who cried out, "This is the Christ... this is the One who is coming"? Jesus could. This is the discernment we want to multiply.

Our freedom as Christians to communicate our message is tied to our defense of others' right to do the same. In our zeal to see a better web, movie, T.V. and general communication industry and environment, we must not deny so many rights that we lose our right to speak through the same media. I think it is at least fair to ask the question, "Would Jesus have been allowed to preach at all in a Jerusalem controlled by orthodox pharisaism?" Did the paganism of the Romans actually contribute to a freer environment for the preaching of the Gospel? We want to be very careful about supporting any movement that seeks to drastically limit a free forum of communication within a nation.

A NOTE TO COMMUNICATION PROFESSIONALS:

I led a public relations work in Washington D.C. in the 80's and my media friends estimated at the time that of approximately 7,000 journalists working there, perhaps 20 or less were Christian. In some ways it was more popular among evangelicals to be a prostitute than a journalist. At least prostitutes were candidates for salvation; journalists were perceived as the "enemy." Things have improved, but this is still a ripe field ready for salt and light.

I have worked with thousands of young people over the last three decades who want to become communication professionals. Because of the environment they have gown up in, they tend to define Christian media work as preaching on T.V. or radio. It is as though we are unable to think of a purpose in media beyond evangelization and church. This is the by-product of split thinking. I often ask people what a Christian wheel would look like. What would a Christian or biblical pilot do? Of course they have a hard time defining a "good" wheel or a "good" pilot because the very thing that makes a good pilot "good" is already a biblical view whether we realize it or not. If we take it a step further to news, entertainment, documentary, or any other area of communication...what does the "Christian" version look like? Are you part of a generation to find out?

CHAPTER 13
Arts and Entertainment

"He has made everything beautiful in its time."

Ecclesiastes 3:11

"One thing I ask of the Lord, this is what I see: that I may dwell in the house of the Lord all the days of my life, to gaze upon the beauty of the Lord and to seek him in his temple."

Psalm 27:4

Everything that God has made is beautiful! Nothing in the universe is without color, form, and design. He turns ashes into beauty. He is the "Song of Songs," the "Potter," the Lord of beauty. He is beautiful. The arts reveal the creator through music, words, color, design, balance, movement, harmony, rhythm. David said that the stars sing the glory of the Lord and there are physicists today who think it is completely possible that the planets do vibrate in perfect harmonic chords. On the seventh day of creation, God rested. We should not think of this rest in terms of tiredness because God does not suffer fatigue. We should think of this rest as taking time to contemplate the beauty of creation, a savoring of the goodness of all that He has made. God's attributes revealed in the arts are beauty, rest, and celebration. God's purpose for this domain is to renew and restore us and give us joy from our labor.

Am I A Christian Artist Or An Artist Who Is Christian?

Christian artists today have a terrible conflict in understanding the purpose of their gift. If their work does not talk about Jesus directly, does it still have value? Can they work on productions with non-Christians? When some see a magnificent building, painting, play or hear a wonderful performance, they are tempted to ask, "Was it produced, created and performed by Christians?" as though that would validate the beauty. But beauty, in and of itself, is an attribute of God. Putting a Jesus sticker on it does not make it more beautiful. Preaching may be beautiful, but beauty does not necessarily preach an additional message. We may have art and beauty in the church, but art does not have to relate directly to ecclesiastical expression in order to reveal God.

Anything, including forms of music, notes, or instruments can be used for good or evil. There is no such thing as demonic notes, rhythms, or instruments. Satan does not own these any more than he owns the moon or mushrooms or color. All these things are an extension of God's creation. Anything that God has made may be used to worship Satan, but it can also be used to reveal God. We tend to think of old music as godly music; anything really new is suspect, if not evil. Of course, this has more to do with personal taste than God. We happily listen to the beautiful Lutheran hymns, content that this music reveals spiritual virtue. What most of us don't know is that Luther put Christian words to the beer garden favorites of the day. I wonder how the German Christians of his day responded to those popular songs being used in church?

Scripture Reveals Three Themes In Music

In the study of the arts and music in scripture, three kinds of musical themes are recorded. Worship, of course, national or political music, and love songs. One love song gets an entire book in the Song of Solomon. Today, worship, hymns, praise and psalms are all important, but we have lost the importance of celebrating human love and love of nation. If you look at the national anthems around the world you will find that the vast majority of them, written before 1970, mention God and His blessing. Until the last century, it was understood that God is involved in the political life of a nation. In the last century, some nations have sought to remove these references to God. Is that because of the secularization of the country or the church's loss of the understanding of God in the political arena? Where are the love songs? Our airwaves are crammed with a message of love that is demeaning or lewd at best. But today, when a musician who is Christian writes and performs a beautiful celebration of human love, we accuse him of being "secular" or not loyal to his faith and not presenting Jesus. Scripture celebrates all these themes of music and uses them to reveal God.

If we define opera as a story put to music, then Moses gives us a very early, if not the first, opera in Deuteronomy 32. It is amazing to think that this national, political leader so understood the importance of music in the life of a nation that, at the end of his life, he would compose a work containing important principles for the people to remember. "And Moses recited the words of this song from beginning to end in the hearing of the whole assembly of Israel..."[1]

The Disciplines Of The Arts

Like science, God rules the arts by laws that govern each discipline; laws of aesthetics, harmony, rhythm, dissonance, color, form, design, positive and negative space. Whether dance, sculpture, painting, writing, or composing, every artist and performer understands that there are principles upon which their discipline is built. Mastering those fundamentals is foundational to their skill. Genius, then, is making those same fundamentals disappear in artistic expression. Unredeemed people create beautiful things because they are created in the image of God. They just do not realize the source of their talent or discipline or their love of beauty. They do not know the gift-giver, but their gift still celebrates God. They are unaware of whom to be grateful to. Whether or not they know God does not make their creation more or less beautiful. Nor do Jewish lyrics make it more beautiful. Beauty has intrinsic value as an extension of God's character and nature.

Lukewarm

So much of what is called Christian music and art today is mediocre at best. Perhaps this is because we think the only thing that matters is

---

1. *Deuteronomy 32:30*

whether it talks about God. It is important to present the message of Christ. However, it is not only absurd, it is dangerous to think that the only thing important about a surgeon is his love of God, that his technical skill in surgery is unimportant. The heart of the individual and the discipline of a craft are two different things and Jesus is Lord of them both. As one who believes in the Creator God, you and I are to value skill as well as right standing with God. We are to celebrate beauty for beauty's sake because He is the Lord of Beauty, the Creator of all skill, and we are to seek the artist's right relationship to Christ, the creator of his gift.[2]

There are no tribes, nations, or cultures without art, music, and sport. Beauty, song, and celebration are all pre-human. They were expressed in God before we existed and they still reveal Him. We don't have to justify the love of sport or art by turning it into an opportunity to talk to the person next to us in the stands about God. We may or may not find that appropriate. It's okay to enjoy talent and God-given gifting for their innate value. It is worship of the Creator, the gift-giver and a celebration of who He is!

STUDY HELP:

Themes to consider when studying and coloring the subject of the arts and entertainment in scripture: *music, design, sport, dance, culture, dress, poetry, literature, crafts, color, sculpture, and beauty.*

The domain of arts and entertainment reveals: **Song of Songs, the Potter**

The primary attribute of God revealed in arts and entertainment: **Beauty**

God governs this domain through: **The laws of aesthetics of each discipline**

The color I used: **Rose**

WORKING VOCATIONAL MISSION STATEMENT:

To provide rest, relaxation and restoration of the soul through beauty and joy.

---

2. *Exodus 3*

A NOTE TO ALL BELIEVERS:

One of my students said that he saw how all the domains related to his personal life in one way or another. But not the arts. What did art and beauty have to do with him? He was not a musician or painter or anything like that. I found this a tragic confession. I responded, "The question you need to ask yourself is, 'Where is the beauty in my life?'" Immediately he teared up. The question touched a deep chord. His life was full of service, duty, devotion, and work...but there was no celebration, beauty, and joy.

This is not uncommon in or out of Christian circles. The world is desperate for beauty. We are so often surrounded by the mundane, thoughtless, chaotic, and ugly. One of the things I love about living in Switzerland is the celebration of beauty in the form of flower boxes on the windows. No matter how humble the farmhouse, every spring color explodes in all the window boxes. This custom serves no practical purpose. These plants can't be eaten. They are just pretty. There is such a need for this understanding of beauty in all of our lives and the life of our communities. Where is the beauty in your life?

My parents were poor and moved from their family homes during the depression to find work in the north of the United States. I was their first child born in a home with an indoor toilet. But from my earliest memory music filled our house. My mother listened to opera on the radio as she washed our hair in the kitchen sink on Saturdays. We never talked about it; there were no music lectures. But it was important to her to have beauty in her very modest home. This is one of the great treasures left to me... the celebration of God in music in my life. We need beauty.

A NOTE TO ARTS AND ENTERTAINMENT PROFESSIONALS:

Whether you are gifted in body, ear or eye, your gift is a celebration of God and a part of the call of God on your life. We have been created by God to need and to celebrate beauty and joy. You are part of God's answer to that world of need. Everything God has made, whether we look at it macroscopically or microscopically, is beautiful and it was all created with sound. So, whether you are celebrating the use of your gift in the work of the church to minister to Christians or to minister to the many who do not go to church, you are ministering Christ. Whether you work with other Christians or non-Christians you are His testimony through your life and skill. You don't have to justify your gift by doing religious material or by kneeling in prayer when you do well, although you may do both. Your gift is justified because it is part of God's nature and character in you. It is part of who He is and how He has made you and the gift itself reveals God. The world needs your gift and the celebration of beauty and joy it brings. Do not hold back! Let's begin the new renaissance.

PART III

OLD TESTAMENT TEMPLATE

IF WE ARE GOING TO DISCIPLE ALL NATIONS

The rebuilding of our Christian minds will take time, effort, and the conviction that we cannot fulfill His vision without it. As I finish writing this volume, I go on to study government from Genesis to Revelation. I pray you are already preparing for what you will apply your own study to.

In this third section I would like to move beyond the domains to other areas of thinking that need to be "reformed." This is not an exhaustive list, but these are the reoccurring needs I see in a decade of teaching this material.

If we are to "finish the task" of reaching and teaching all nations, we are going to need a bigger picture of who Christ is. Today we love Him. The first apostles were stunned by Him. We are going to need God to change our concept and definition of nations to His. Otherwise we will fight for the "traditions of men" rather than the will of God. We must become aware of the ever-present dangers that accompany any power. The Kingdom strategy is always a servant strategy. We will have to embrace, and even love and seek, radical change as a lifestyle.

Welcome to the 21st Century!

CHAPTER 14
We Need a Supreme Christ

If believers are to regain the influence God designed for us in every arena of life, we are going to need a greater revelation of Christ. One of the most important questions in the New Testament, one Jesus was continually leading people to ask, was, "Who are You?" The great transforming truths of the gospel are all contained in the answer to that one question. "Who is Jesus Christ?" Like me, you probably feel as though you've known the answer to that question since you were saved.

You say, "Jesus is the Son of God, born of a virgin and through His death on the cross and the forgiveness of my sin, He is the Savior of my soul." And as far as it goes, you are accurate. When our minds are split between secular and sacred we think the gospel is primarily concerned with the sacred, things of a spiritual nature, eternal things, heavenly things... things that are holy. We feel we know who Jesus is. But this is a very "small" Jesus. If we are going to regain greater influence as a generation of Christians, we are going to have to wrestle with His identity, as Paul did with the Colossians. Let's look at the size of Paul's Jesus:

Colossians 1:15-20
15 He is the image of the invisible God, the firstborn over all creation.
16 For by him all things were created: things in heaven and on earth, visible and invisible, whether thrones or powers or rulers or authorities; all things were created by him and for him.
17 He is before all things, and in him all things hold together.
18 And he is the head of the body, the church; he is the beginning and the firstborn from among the dead, so that in everything he might have the supremacy.

19 For God was pleased to have all his fullness dwell in him,
20 and through him to reconcile to himself all things, whether things
on earth or things in heaven, by making peace through his blood, shed
on the cross.

Look at the letter from Paul to the believers in Colosse. What questions were the readers dealing with that Paul is answering? In this letter he states his desires for the Colossians very clearly by telling what he has been praying constantly for them:

Colossians 1:9-14

9 For this reason, since the day we heard about you, we have not stopped praying for you and asking God to fill you with the knowledge of his will through all spiritual wisdom and understanding.
10 And we pray this in order that you may live a life worthy of the Lord and may please him in every way: bearing fruit in every good work, growing in the knowledge of God,
11 being strengthened with all power according to his glorious might so that you may have great endurance and patience, and joyfully
12 giving thanks to the Father, who has qualified you to share in the inheritance of the saints in the kingdom of light.
13 For he has rescued us from the dominion of darkness and brought us into the kingdom of the Son he loves,
14 in whom we have redemption, the forgiveness of sins.

The Colossians have been converted. They know Christ in a personal way and they love the Spirit.[1] They have been faithfully pastored in these things by Epaphras, their minister. But Paul desires deeply for them to move beyond these basic foundations of the gospel that have been laid in their lives. He wants them to grow from salvation into knowledge of the will of God, having wisdom and understanding in their daily lives. He wants them to learn what will make them effective in "every good work." He wants them to grow in the knowledge of God so that they may demonstrate through their lives the difference between the "kingdom of light" and the "domain of darkness" which they have been saved from.

---

1. *Colossians 1:6-8*

He wants their "salvation" to get feet and start being walked out in everything they do.

What is important here is that the very first thing Paul focuses on, in order to accomplish this greater maturing growth in the Colossians' lives, is the answer to the question "Who is Jesus?" They know Him as Savior. They know Him as the One who sends the Comforter in the person of the Holy Spirit. But that is not enough! He is more! If they are going to "live a life worthy" of Him, they are going to need a greater revelation of His absolute supremacy over everything! Our soul? Yes. Our spirits? Yes. Heaven? Yes. The invisible world? Yes. And *more*! Look at how Paul labors with them to understand. How can he spell it out any more clearly?

The Lord Of All!

Christ created *all things*! All things in heaven and *on earth*! He created *everything*, invisible and *visible*! All things were created for Him and He ranks as commanding officer of *all things*! Are you getting the point? He is *supreme* in *everything*! What does this mean? This means there is no such thing as a "secular" and a "sacred" world. All things belong to Christ. This means the temporal things of life are not less important than the eternal things of life...because *all* things belong to Christ. This means the gospel is not about salvation alone and how Christ saves us. The message is also about God's reconciling power in every area of our lives, families, communities, and nations. What has the cross of Christ, the blood of Jesus, reconciled? Everything! Everything on earth and everything in heaven. Christ has made peace with every part of His creation through Jesus. He is not at war with any part of it. My little brain *barely knows* how to think about this Jesus.

What Paul is saying to us in Colossians is that Jesus is Lord of everything. He is Lord of the so-called "spiritual" and the material world. He is Lord of salvation and all social concerns. He is supreme over the eternal and the temporal. He is King of heaven and of earth. Because He is Lord of all, there is no such thing as the "secular." Because all things were created *by* Him and *for* Him, they all belong *to* Him. He is the rightful heir to all that is; and He has shed His blood to see it all reconciled.

The Message Is The Kingdom

This means when we preach salvation alone we are missing the majority of God's kingdom message. Salvation is essential. There is no other way into the Kingdom of God. But salvation is the *entry* into the Kingdom; it is not the goal or the Kingdom itself. By making it the goal we have lost most of God's message. We cannot "bear fruit in every good work" because with salvation alone we cannot grow "in the knowledge of God" in the rest of life. We cannot be "strengthened with all power" because we do not have the "knowledge of His will through all spiritual wisdom and understanding." Therefore, we are the largest church in history, but the weakest church when it comes to actually influencing the lives, communities, and nations we have reached.

We must destroy the split thinking we have been taught and take up again the gospel of the Kingdom. Then, and only then, will not only our words, but our actions and influence bear witness to the absolute supremacy of Christ and His message. How do we do this? How do we restore our Christian minds? How do we get the gospel of the Kingdom back?

There Are Only Two Kingdoms

It seems to me that a careful study of the Word of God reveals two Kingdoms and therefore, what we would call today, two world-views. In one view, Jesus is Lord of everything, and in the other He is not. In God's view of reality, everything is integrated under His supreme authority. All other world-views have a split view of reality, that is to say, that one part of creation is more real than another. In philosophy, this debate uses the language of "the one and the many," particulars vs. ideal. Scientists talk about the material vs. immaterial, visible vs. invisible. In theological language, we discuss this dichotomy in terms of temporal vs. eternal, heavenly vs. earthly. Existentialism puts its emphasis on the unseen world, Communism on the seen. Hinduism, Buddhism, and Islam say the earthly is unreal – reality is in the unseen world. Rationalism says if I can measure it, it is real. The God of the Bible says there is no "versus." It all belongs to Him. All that has been made is from

Him and to Him and reconciled to Him through the shed blood of Jesus Christ. This is what Paul is struggling to convey in Colossians 1, and every other New Testament writer in the exploding Gentile and Jewish churches.

The only way we can live in the Kingdom of light is by integrating all that comes under the Lordship of Jesus Christ. We must remarry the elements of God's Kingdom that have been estranged through split thinking. We must dispel the darkness of our minds by refusing the concept of secular and sacred, the dualism of a lost world. God is not just or merciful. He is just *and* merciful. He is not either the God of heaven or earth. He is the God of heaven *and* earth. God does not care more for the invisible than the visible, the unseen than the seen. He is the Lord of science and prayer. God is not only redeeming His human creation, He is redeeming His material creation. He cares for every bird, species, and plant He has made. God is not alienated from our ecological concerns; He is the author and the perfecter of them. This Christ does not turn a blind eye to earthly justice, preferring heavenly. He suffers with those who suffer and calls on His people to give voice to the silenced.

Keys To Greatness In The Kingdom

In Matthew 5, Jesus reveals the keys of greatness in the Kingdom of Heaven. He says we are to integrate the teaching of the Law and the Prophets with His teaching of grace, the cross, and the Holy Spirit, and that "whoever practices and teaches these commands will be called great in the kingdom of heaven."[2]

Matthew 5:17-19
17 "Do not think that I have come to abolish the Law or the Prophets; I have not come to abolish them but to fulfill them.
18 I tell you the truth, until heaven and earth disappear, not the smallest letter, not the least stroke of a pen, will by any means disappear from the Law until everything is accomplished.
19 Anyone who breaks one of the least of these commandments and teaches others to do the same will be called least in the kingdom of

---

2. *Matthew 4:19*

148

heaven, but whoever practices and teaches these commands will be called great in the kingdom of heaven."

Matthew 13:52
And he said to them, 'Therefore every teacher of the law who has been instructed about the kingdom of heaven is like the owner of a house who brings out of his storeroom new treasures as well as old.'

If we do not integrate the Old with the New Testament, if we do not preach the old and the new, if we do not integrate the spiritual and material, the heavenly and the earthly, the seen and the unseen, then we are not seeing the real Jesus.

CHAPTER 15
We Need God's View Of Nations

"Ask of me, and I will make the nations your inheritance, the ends of the earth your possession."

Psalm 2:8

"After this I looked and there before me was a great multitude that no one could count, from every nation, tribe, people and language, standing before the throne and in front of the Lamb. They were wearing white robes and were holding palm branches in their hands. And they cried out in a loud voice: "Salvation belongs to our God who sits on the throne, and to the Lamb."

Revelation 7:9-10

To regain the influence God desires for the body of Christ on earth we need God's view of nations. We must look again at scripture to see the destiny of the Church in relation to God's whole plan and purpose. What is our destiny here on planet earth? We often pray, "Thy will be done on earth as it is in heaven." What would the will of the Father look like on earth? Let's begin by looking at what it is not.

Our destiny is not salvation

God died to save us and desires salvation for all. The only way into the Kingdom of God is through Jesus Christ, but salvation is not God's ultimate goal. The new birth is a means to an end. When we do not preach the whole word of God we produce hopelessness. We leave people with a dream of heaven, and no sense of their destiny here on earth. When we go to the whole world and preach salvation alone, we neglect the rest of God's plan.

Our destiny in God is not to be filled with the Holy Spirit

God's power in the Holy Spirit is a wonderful and essential thing – God the comforter come to live within us. We cannot thrive without Him. But His filling is not our goal. Again, the tools of the Holy Spirit are a means to an end, not the end in themselves. People who come into the Kingdom and go from meeting to meeting to get renewed and filled with the Spirit are cheating themselves. God has more, much more! The coming of the Holy Spirit is part of God's great river that is to move us out. He is the empowerment to take off...but to where?

Our destiny is not miracles

God did create the cosmos. He did part the Red Sea. Jesus did feed four and five thousand with a few fish and a little bread. But each of these miracles teach us something specifically. They are a means to God's end. If we do not understand a miracle's lesson, then we are like the disciples in the boat with Jesus.[1] They saw the boy and the fish and the bread. They saw the five thousand. They held the bread. They broke the bread and passed it out. They picked up the leftovers and put them in twelve huge baskets. They see, taste, touch, and eat the miracle food. Then hours later they are in the boat with Jesus and one of them notes that he forgot the bread. Jesus rebukes them and says "O ye of little faith." They saw, they tasted, they experienced the miracle, but they did not understand what God was teaching them through it. The result was that when they got in the boat they had nothing – no bread, no understanding. A miracle always points us to something about the nature and character of God and how He wants us to think. They are God's way of preparing us, but for what?

---

1. Matthew 16

Our destiny is not churches

Churches are essential to God's plan, but they are not His goal. God's strategy is not to have all His people in church 24/7. God's desire is to use church to prepare His people to carry out their work. But what is the work?

The Four Thousand Year Mandate

For 4,000 years God has been trying to reveal our destiny to us. Before the fall, after the fall, right through Jesus and Revelation, God is clarifying His "will on earth." What purpose has God created us for? In His likeness, as His people what is our destiny in this life? As we enter this 5th millennium in His plan we are still unclear.

Adam-Abraham-Jesus

To Adam, God said, "Be fruitful and increase in number; fill the earth and subdue it."[2] Some translations read, "take dominion" others "cultivate the earth." The root word for "cultivate" is "cultos" the same root word as for "culture." In essence God is saying, "Fill the earth and create tribes, nations, peoples...cultures." To Abraham, he says "I am going to make you as the sand of the sea, I am going to make you as the stars of the sky.[3] I am going to multiply you and through you I will bless all nations.[4] Multiply! Cultivate! Then through His Son, Jesus, the Father repeats His mandate. "Reach every creature."[5] Multiply! "Teach all nations."[6] Cultivate! For 4,000 years God has repeated our destiny again and again. Our destiny as the people of God is: Christ revealed in the nations. In order to understand this, in order to enter into our full inheritance on earth we must understand nations from God's perspective.

We understand the need to "reach" the nations. We understand that there is a huge unreached population in the 10/40 window and that we must target these nations. We understand that we must send workers to

---

2. *Genesis 1:28*
3. *Genesis 22:17*
4. *Genesis 22:18*
5. *Mark 16:15*
6. *Luke 24:47*

tribes and languages which have no witness. When we see 20 percent or 50 percent of the population converted and the church planted we have a tendency to see our work as coming to completion. But this is only the beginning.

What Is A "Nation?"

What is God's view of nations? What is God trying to convey to us in His word about his purpose for tribes and peoples? To understand God's heart for the nations we have to start at the beginning...Genesis. If you mark your Bible every time the word *nation* is mentioned, you will begin to think you are reading a book that is all about nations. God speaks about community and nations more than any other single subject. Nations are emphasized at the beginning and at the end as they all gather before the throne of God. Before the fall, God intended man to fill every corner of the earth and to develop cultures and nations. After the fall, the plan continues. In Genesis chapter 10, we begin to see the celebration of nations. You can almost feel God's excitement as He recounts the multiplication of tribes, each with their own language, culture, and land. God loves diversity. He loves multiplication. He loves this massive process of migration and re-establishment of new people groups. God is so pleased with the concept of creating nations that every time someone gets wounded or hurt he blesses them by promising that He will make them a new people, tribe and nation.

A New Nation Is A Blessing

As God calls Abraham out of His homeland he promises that He is going to make him the father of a great "family of nations." When Ishmael is thrown from his father's tribe, God says, "Don't worry Ishmael, I have a blessing for you too." And what is the blessing? "Ishmael, I am going to make you a family of nations." " I am going to create twelve great nations through you." Lot is abused in his new homeland and as he leaves in defeat God encourages him. "Lot, I am going to make you into two nations." Can you feel the heart of God? God is excited. He is doing what He loves. He is multiplying people in His image *and creating new nations*. When Rebecca is very pregnant, God speaks encouragement to her. "You carry two nations in your womb, Rebecca." God's expectation was that being allowed to parent a new nation was an honor. He is using them to accomplish something very dear to His heart. What does He love? He loves people and nations, lots of nations each with their own language, culture, and land.

Empires Are Not A Blessing

In chapter 11 of Genesis we come to the story of the Tower of Babel. I have heard many messages on Babel, but never one on what appears to me to be the real sin. We often focus on the tower they wanted to build to heaven and the pride of that aspiration. We see it as using science and technology to exalt themselves over God. But the tower of Babel is only the symbol of their sin, not the sin itself. What is it in this account that moves God to action? In verse 4 the Babylonians say, "Come, let us build ourselves a city, with a tower that reaches to the heavens, so that we may make a name for ourselves and not be scattered over the face of the whole earth." Babylon wanted to be a "mega nation." They wanted to stop the great migration of peoples, gather on a plain in Shinar, and build one great nation with one language, one culture, and one government. They wanted to be the most powerful nation on the face of the earth. God's plan was for multiplication and diversity and the Babylonians wanted an empire. God defeats their ambitions. They are defeated in their purpose as every empirical dream of domination is defeated in history. God is determined to continue to multiply and create nations.

Nations Are Not Targets

For God, nations are not targets for evangelism, they are strategies for revealing God Himself. Nations are not convenient ways to divide up the work, or subheadings to the mission task. Nations were in the heart of God when He created the universe and nations are there before His throne for all eternity. God's plan of redemption is for individuals, but it is also a reconciliation plan for nations.

As God moves on in Genesis from the origins of the cosmos, man, family, and nations, He tells us the details of the origin of one nation. Using Israel as His model, He reveals His plans for human culture. God says to Abraham, "I will teach you and you will teach the nations."[7] To Isaac God repeats, "I will bless you and you will bless the nations."[8] To Moses in the wilderness, "I will give you these understandings of how to be a nation and through these I will bless all nations."[9] God says that He is choosing Israel because they are a small and undeveloped people. His principles applied will make them the greatest nation on the face of the earth. He can use them to reveal Himself in and through all nations. He makes Israel the template of what He wants for all peoples, in all nations, in all of time.

All The Prophets Prophesied To Nations

If we focus on the prophets, all 17 of them prophesied to nations. Every one of them has God's word for at least one nation, many of them for more. Today, prophecy is often focused on the individual or the church. This is not wrong, but it was not the focus of the prophets in scripture. What does it mean that a simple shepherd like Amos in Israel has a bigger understanding of God's strategy in nations than we seem to have today?

When we read of the parting of the Red Sea and God's miraculous defeat of the Egyptian army on behalf of Israel, we are not only reading of God's heart for the Jewish nation, we are reading of God's heart for all nations. We are seeing the lengths to which God will go for a people. We are seeing God move heaven and earth in order to preserve His revelation of Himself in a people. That is not God's message for *one* nation. He is saying to *all* nations "I will bless you, so that all nations of the world will be blessed." It is God's desire that they be free, that they have their land, that they have the right to learn the blessings of God and become examples of the greatness of God.

---

7. *Genesis 12:3; 18:18; 22:8*
8. *Genesis 26:3-5*
9. *Deuteronomy 4:5-8*

Nations Are Miracles

Nations are miracles. They are birthed by the will of God; they have their origins in the creator. They cannot exist but by His will. God has made a covenant with every people and that covenant stands until that people so breaks the covenant that it can no longer stand. God said to Israel, "You may destroy these nations, but you may not destroy this nation, because I have a covenant with them." God will remove the rights of a nation that has become cancerous. This is not His desire and purpose; He wants to reach and disciple those nations.

Jesus Picks Up Where The Prophets Left Off

As we move on to the New Testament Jesus picks up the 2000 year old theme and says, "Multiply, disciple all nations." The vision that begins with Adam does not change. God's purpose for all peoples continues through the Good News of righteousness in Jesus Christ. In Matthew, Jesus says, "Do not think that I have come to destroy or eliminate the laws of Moses. I have not come to destroy them; I have come to fulfill them. And anyone who does not preach these laws and principles will be the least in the Kingdom of God. But anyone who preaches and lives the principles will be great in the Kingdom of God."[10] Jesus is saying that the coming of salvation does not eliminate the need to teach and preach the principles of how to live in my community and how to disciple my nation. We must preach salvation and we must teach nation building. When we preach only the New Testament we are discipling people in being "least in the Kingdom." It is good that they are in the Kingdom, but God wants more; God desires to release influence and "greatness in the Kingdom." For this we must return to discipling with the whole Bible.

Recently, I received an e-mail from Argentina. The leaders of the revival there sent out a letter asking forgiveness of the body of Christ worldwide, saying that in their zeal for evangelism and church planting they had failed to address the issues of justice and economics. They felt partly responsible for the national crisis in both these areas. This is a humble response to a devastating fact: we have lost much of God's thinking. We

---

10. *Matthew 5*

reach the nations, but we leave them in injustice, disease, illiteracy, and poverty. We no longer have the keys of greatness in the Kingdom that bring blessing to the community. That is the bad news. The good news is that God wants us to re-inherit those keys in our generation.

Paul Grasps God's Heart For The Nations

I believe that Paul is the primary architect and author of the New Testament because He understood nations from God's perspective. Some of the apostles wanted Christianity to be a subset of Jewish culture. Paul contests them and says that the Good News of Christ is not to be a subset of any culture. It is God's message for all nations and is to be expressed in and through their languages and cultures in their own way. If Paul had not won this argument you and I would be singing Jewish songs and dancing Jewish dances. But Paul did win, and so won the right for the diversity of God to be revealed through all peoples in all times.

Nations, Tribes, And Peoples Are Eternal

In Revelation we are given a picture of God's throne and the throng standing before Him. How are they gathered? By denominations? No. By families? No. By nations! Nationhood is eternal. It is part of the New Jerusalem. Multiculturalism is celebrated for all time. Nations express the very diversity of God and His nature. In the new earth we come in all our national glory, laying our treasures of justice, health, wisdom, love, beauty and wealth before His feet, declaring Him the source of all that we have that is good. The Kings bring the glory of their nations before the throne.[11]

To this day, the Jews have failed to understand that their blessing and destiny as a nation lay in the blessing and destiny of all nations. And it seems, as Christians, we do not understand this either. God is not after a big church only; He is looking for a diverse church and a deep church. He desires to save individuals and reach nations, but also to teach them and bring a demonstration of the Glory of His truth on earth. How do we do this? It is all in the Book. Moses' job was to teach the smallest, poorest, most destitute people in history about God and science, God and justice,

---

11. *Revelation 7:4-10*

God and economics, God and family, God and worship, God and wisdom, God and beauty, God and health...in other words, God and all of life. This revelation was learning to think as God thinks and live as God would live in our place. Moses wrote it all down in the five books of the Law so that the Jewish people, and all peoples of all nations, would have the keys to the blessings of the Kingdom.

How do we make great nations for the Kingdom of God? We give them the whole counsel of God. What a message! What a God! A God for all nations.

CHAPTER 16
We Need A Biblical View of Vocations

"For we are God's workmanship, created in Christ Jesus to do good works, which God prepared in advance for us to do."

Ephesians 2:10

"God blessed them and said to them, 'Be fruitful and increase in number, fill the earth and subdue it."

Genesis 1:28

I love to watch children. They are such a great microcosm of our own adult social and physical concerns. They play out life on the surface without inhibition or subtlety. In watching children, I often understand others and myself better. Children know what they love and love what they are made to do. They will, in a free environment of creativity, play out their God-given gifts. A coworker told me of his daughter, about age three, stopping him as he left for work. She admonished that what he was wearing didn't match, and began a morning routine that would last for years of picking out his clothes. She was good. Her sense of color, fashion, and flare was all there at the age of three! Another friend of mine, now the scheduler for a nation's cabinet minister, as a child would create a make-believe desk complete with phone, agenda, and calculator and proceed to make fantasy airline reservations. I used to create a little podium and draw all my friends in to give them speeches. From early in life it was clear that my future would involve talking. Children, created in the image of God, know they are gifted and they love what they are created to do.

Work Is Worship

If we are to reveal the Kingdom in all its glory, we need God's perspective on vocations and work. A large part of how we "know and enjoy Him forever" is in fulfilling the work He created us to do. We reveal God, in part, through the work of our hands. Just as God reveals Himself through His creation, our work reveals who we are, what we believe, and whom and what we worship. One of the most demeaning experiences for human beings is believing they have nothing to contribute or having their contribution devalued or denied. God gave six days to the worship of work and one to rest.

In our focus on evangelism, missions, traditional church ministry, and the secular versus sacred dichotomy we have nearly lost the theology of the laity, or a Godly perspective of work outside of the institution of the church. When I first came to missions in the early 70's we lamented the "funeral services" churches often had for those "laying down their lives" for missions. We thought missionary service was the greatest calling on earth. We thought God had released us into what He had made us to do. Today, in ministry circles, we tend to have our own kind of "funeral services" for those poor souls who are going back into "secular" work, just getting a job. Having broken the blindness to the call of God in missions we, in missions, developed a new blindness to the call of God to the rest of society.

Tom Marshall estimated that perhaps 20 percent of God's people are called into the ecclesiastical work of the Church. The other 80 percent are called into other vocations to serve God's Kingdom. Over the last century we have devalued work outside the church to the point that much of the body of Christ feels they did not get the good gifts like preaching or evangelism. They sit in pews around the world wishing they could really serve God. Our vision for a businessperson is to make money for missions or the church building program. Leaders might serve as church treasurer. Our goal for teachers is the church Sunday school program. Communicators? Well, we have church newsletters and bulletin boards that need preparing. Artists, musicians, and entertainers are always needed in worship and outreach programs. They might help create worship banners too.

Scientists, technicians? Those are tough ones. Fix the church plumbing or buses? Do the engineering for our construction program? Political leaders and lawyers really stretch the imagination for service. The result of this thinking is that most of God's people go to work five or six days a week to make money and wait for Sunday when they can do something for God. How tragic! No wonder we are a church that lacks influence. Once we walk outside the doors of the sanctuary we have no idea what we are to do for the Kingdom of God. What we have lost is a theology of work and God's purposes in all giftings. If we are to regain the historic influence of believers in their communities we will have to regain God's view of all the vocations.

Who Secularized What?

I want to make a radical proposition. Today, we talk a great deal about the secularization of societies. Christmas, church, Sunday, etc. And it is true, much of culture, even religious culture has been turned into a business venture void of additional meaning. Who is responsible for that secularization process? Many believers sound as though they think the lost, those who do not know God, are to blame. But that cannot be true. They are just lost. They do not know God and do not have the ability to change. They do live in a secular world because their world does not have the living God. Believers, on the other hand, have a choice! We can refuse secularization because God is in the picture. But society is hopelessly secularized when those who know God, when those who are called by His name, take God out of most of life and most of their work. When we as believers have left God out of our jobs, when we only go to work to make money, then the salt has lost all flavor. When the "light of the world" is dim, it is dark indeed. We, as Christians, are the salt and light. We are the problem and the solution.

God's View Of The Vocations

When God created the cosmos he gave the human race a very specific and wonderful part in His whole design. We are made by God to steward

His material world and to create human culture that reveals the full image of God. His mandate in Genesis 1:28, isn't for us to be farmers, it's for us to use our gifts to create according to His image upon each of us. Some of us reveal Jehovah Jireh, God the Provider, through our entrepreneurial and business gifts. Some of us, in our passion for justice and service for others, work to create and serve the community through the justice system. Some of us are literally compelled by God to make life more beautiful, visually and audibly. Our passion is to reveal the God of beauty. Others, who have a passion for truth and knowledge, become communicators and educators. Some who are dying to discover become scientists and explorers, those who go to the ends of the world, cosmos and our reality to learn what God has made. Still more have a passion to reveal the Father God by raising future generations to know and enjoy Him forever. And others desire to help everyone know God better and to be aware of the worship of their lives, families, and work. We seek to reveal the Great High Priest in ministry to the whole body. Our gifts are different, but everyone is gifted to reveal God in their life and talents.

Real Cameos

I have the great privilege of traveling God's planet and meeting His people. Sometimes the thought of getting on one more airplane seems unbearable. But it is never tiring to be in a new culture with a new body of believers. God's diversity is exhilarating. From all over the world I have cameos of God's people affected by the loss of our vocational revelation. There is the successful Swedish businessman who wept as we talked about God's call on business. He said that all his life he had known somehow this vision for business was true, but he had never heard it validated by the church. An English medical student read this material on my web page and wrote to say that she had intended quitting medical school because she deeply wanted to serve God. Now, she understood that being a doctor was her service for God. There is the sanitation engineer who broke down and wept when he heard the vocational mandate of science. He said that no one in the Christian community had ever validated his work to keep his community healthy. His missionary brother was honored every time he visited church with him. This was the first time his work had been said to be valuable in God's eyes. An Indian business-man almost leapt with joy at the good news that business ability was a gift of God. Some Christians in India have developed a vocation caste system; business is considered the lowest caste. There is the South African believer who found for the first time that his job of redeveloping old mining compounds into livable communities was a holy calling. He had been assigned millions in tax funds to turn these symbols of injustice and greed that were, in part, to blame for the destruction of family structure in the black community into something that provided quality of life. He was shocked at how much instruction there was for his job in scripture. In an interview for a Swiss Christian magazine I was asked, "What would you say to those who are convinced that a believer cannot be involved in politics today without dirtying their hands and compromising their witness?" This is far from an isolated concept.

If we are to become a church of influence we must embrace God's perspective of all the vocational callings! This means a reformation of our thinking about the laity or those who are called to serve God in the community outside the church structure. In order to restore God's view of work we must have God's view of the importance of community and our role as Christians in serving it. Jesus summarizes the whole of the Law and the Prophets into two commandments: "'Love the Lord your God with all your heart and with all your soul and with all your mind.' This is the first and greatest commandment. And the second is like it: 'Love your neighbor as yourself.'"[1] He is radically emphasizing God and community as our focus. We need a generation that will become so saturated in the Word of God that they can again articulate God's purpose for every arena of life.

Vocational Missions Mandates

The Hippocratic Oath, while not Christian in origin, led the thinking and commitment of medical doctors around the world for more than 2000 years. What might be the result of the world's largest body of believers getting a hold of God's thinking on all of God's work? What would happen if every Christian in the world began to do their work as though it was the call of God and his or her service to the Kingdom? What would hap-

---

1. *Matthew 22:37-39*

pen if, inspired by the Holy Spirit, we began to take an oath for justice, an oath for education, an oath for media, an oath for science that serves? Is it possible that the only thing our communities need is for Christians to stop being secular? Is it possible that the darkness of the world is really nothing at all, and all that is needed is for the light of believers to shine?

I have a dream. In this vision of the future, I see a generation who can articulate and apply God's view of civil justice, economics, science, education, family, the arts, communication, and church ministry. I see a generation of believers who grew up believing what they love to do is a gift from God and who desire with all their hearts to use these talents in the service of God and their community. I dream of these young people taking oaths to their specific callings in dedication services all over the Christian world. And yes, I will say it, I dream of a generation who is willing to die for the Lord of justice, provision and freedom.

In my search for the Kingdom I have pursued men and women of God who seemed to see the same deficits I saw in the impact of the church. In chapter 4 I told you of Tom Marshall, the New Zealand pastor with an enormous vision of the Kingdom of God, speaking on our campus in Hawaii, I wept for hours with a broken heart over our diminished gospel message. After his message I prayed, "God, you must show us the road back. You must reveal again your great revelations of Kingdom life beyond salvation." That was ten years ago.

A Call To Develop A Practical Theology Of Every Domain

After ten years of studying the scriptures with vocations and community in mind, I have my first simplistic run at articulating the vocational missions mandate. God's purpose in and through the domain of:

Government: Justice – King of Kings
Is to provide an independent and objective source of arbitration and conflict resolution for society and between nations, providing and insuring justice and equity for all its citizens.

Family: Nurture and Love – The Heavenly Father
Is to provide a safe, loving and nurturing environment for the growth, values, and education of the next generation.

Church: Mercy and Holiness – The Great High Priest
Is to provide for propagation of the faith and discipleship of all believers in the whole nature and character of God, His Word applied to the work and walk of faith, and to facilitate the expression of that faith in worship, fellowship and the sacraments of the church.

Science and Technology: Order and Power – The Creator
Is to discover and use God's natural laws in order to bless all creation by pursuing a higher quality of life, better health, and greater stewardship of God's resources and created universe.

Economics and Business: Provision – God our Provider
Is to provide the needed goods and services and gainful employment opportunities for the community at large at a fair market price and wage.

Education: Knowledge – The Great Teacher
Is to develop the God-given gifts in every person to their highest potential in the service of their community, believing God gifts every child.

Communication and Media: Truth – The Living Word
Is to provide truthful, objective information of importance to the community at large so that citizens can make informed decisions.

Arts and Entertainment: Beauty – The Potter, The Song of Songs
Is to provide for rest, relaxation, and renewal of the soul through beauty and joy.

This is only a start. We must all work together for God's reformation of a generation.

"Thy Kingdom come," Lord, "on earth as it is in heaven."

CHAPTER 17
We Need Biblical Strategies:
The Wilderness Temptations

"No temptation has seized you except what is common to man."

1 Corinthians 1:13

"For we do not have a high priest who is unable to sympathize with our weaknesses, but we have one who has been tempted in every way just as we are... yet was without sin."

Hebrews 4:15

Jesus faced three temptations in the wilderness. The incident in His life is important enough that three of the apostles include it in their account.[1] For many years I have looked at these three temptations, asking for greater personal revelation of how they work themselves out in my life. Jesus said that *every* temptation is common to everyone and that he suffered them *all*, just as you and I do.[2]   It seems to me, then, that the biblical emphasis in His life on these three temptations must mean they are significant for you and me as well. If we are to regain our Christ-like influence in our communities, it is essential that we understand the temptations we face.

Three Temptations – Three Strategies

In the Matthew 4 account we are given a setting, a word of temptation from the devil, and God's word that Jesus uses to counter the attack. Each of the three elements is vital in understanding the text and the temptation. We begin with, "Then Jesus was led by the Spirit..." vs. 4:1. This opening shocks me. It plays with my preconceived ideas of what it feels like when

---

1. *Matthew 4:1-11; Mark 1:12-13; Luke 4:1-13*
2. *1 Corinthians 10:13; Hebrews 2:18*

the Spirit of God is active in my life. No matter how often I read to the contrary in scripture, I think *being led by the Spirit will feel great! It will take me to wonderful places.*

Matthew says that He was led "into the desert," vs. 4:1. Into the desert? I thought God's Spirit was supposed to lead us into the Promised Land, into peace, love, joy, and the abundant life. Well...the Spirit also led Jesus into a wilderness. I hate it, but that is what God's Word says.

The Holy Spirit's purpose in taking Jesus there was "...to be tempted by the devil" vs. 4:1. He was not tempted because Satan had it in for Him. He was not tempted because He had sin in His life. God lead Jesus into purposeful strategic temptation to prepare Him for the call on His life. The devil was involved, but God was the active agent in this situation.

"After fasting for forty days and forty nights..." vs. 4:2. After! When He is hungry, weak, isolated, and vulnerable in every way, that is when the attack comes. The Spirit of God has led Him to fast, led Him to the wilderness, led Him to vulnerability and then allows, even initiates, the accuser of His soul coming at that moment? This tests our understanding of the character and ways of God. Even though we say His strength is proved in our weakness, we still think attacks will come when we are strong. Even though we say we must decrease so that He may increase, we think spiritual maturity will mean we are stronger.

Matthew goes on to say, "He was hungry" vs. 4:2. The simple, infuriating humanity of Jesus. It rebukes us when we want to be more than human. It stares back at us when we would have the world see us as invincible and strong. The shear human need He suffered humiliates our desire to have no needs.

Temptation One: His Identity In The Face Of Physical Need

In this setting of severe and abject physical need in the wilderness, "The tempter came to him and said, 'If you are the Son of God, tell these stones to become bread.'" Be careful here. What is the temptation? Can God turn stones into bread? Of course. That does not tempt the power of God. Does God want to provide for His children? Yes! Does He care about their basic physical needs? Of course. A child does not ask for bread and a loving father give a stone. Neither God's power nor His love of His children are being tested here. But something much more subtle. Something far more human.

The key here is the word "If..." "*If* you are the Son of God..." vs. 4:3. Jesus is being tempted to doubt His identity. In the face of desperate physical need, legitimate need; when Jesus does not have what every human being needs and must have to survive; needing what God himself has created every human being to have; in this desperate and destitute state, the devil says, "*If* you are the Son of God...." Meaning, "Are you the Son of God?" You hungry, thirsty, bag of bones, heap of filth. Really? You are the beloved, full of power, Messiah? You? Well, if you are, *prove it*! Do a little miracle for me, dude. Demonstrate a little of that galactic power. Feed yourself. Produce a little miracle bread...*if* you can."

Later in His life of ministry, at least two of Jesus' public miracles are creating miraculous amounts of bread. But that is not the test of the moment. Neither is whether or not He can, or will go a little longer in the face of physical need. The test here is to doubt who He is in God, to doubt His Sonship, His inheritance, His acceptability to the Father in the face of physical need. That is the first temptation.

Jesus does not fall for this subtle test of His identity. He responds, "It is written, 'Man does not live by bread alone...'" vs. 4:4. Jesus does not deny that He is hungry. He does not deny that He, like every other man, needs bread. He does not fall into debate over God's ability or willingness to provide what is needed. He simply acknowledges that bread is not our only need. And He goes on to quote more scripture, "... but by every word that comes from the mouth of God." vs. 4:4. Every word! Not just *some* of God's truths, but all of them, including God's word recorded just five verses later, "This is my Son, whom I love. With him I am well pleased," Matt. 3:17. The word had been spoken through the prophets, the angels, the wise men, Elizabeth, Mary, Joseph, a voice from Heaven. Jesus would not doubt the truth of these words because He was facing physical need. The enemy is defeated by Christ standing on the truth of His Father's words about who He is. End of round one!

Temptation Two: Identity And The Need To Demonstrate Spiritual Authority

Round two! A new setting. The devil takes Jesus to the Holy City and stands Him on the highest point of the temple. How did he do that? Was it a vision? Was it transport of the kind Philip experienced in Acts 8:39-40? We don't know. Jesus is experiencing a manifestation of some sort. He was in one place, the wilderness, and now He is on the pinnacle of the temple. What a heady sensation that must have been. What an adrenaline rush. The setting has been transformed now from one of physical need to one of spiritual heights. Satan has taken Him to the holy city, the holy temple, the center of religion, and the heights of earthly "spiritual" symbols.

Here Satan says: "If you are the Son of God..." vs. 4:6. The same words! Is it the same temptation? Yes! But this setting is no longer in the context of physical need and weakness. Now Jesus is in the midst of spiritual exaltation. He is high and lifted up, looking down on His Holy City from the pinnacle of the temple, tempted to doubt His identity in the Father, tempted to doubt that He is the Son, and if He does believe that He is the Son, tempted to prove it. This is His chance to demonstrate to everyone's satisfaction who He is. He can show them now.

This is a powerful temptation. If you have ever served God, you have experienced this temptation. Somehow, the hand of God or the hand of Satan has raised you to a place of prominence, a place of being "seen" by others in ministry. On one hand, you experience joy that you can serve God in a great way. You have a genuine desire to use this exposure to help people more effectively. But there is always something else stirring inside, an inner dialogue that prods, challenges, and nags. "How did you get here?" "Do you really think God can use you?" "Others probably think you are a fool." "Hey, you got the goods? Prove it! Do something spectacular..." The temptation is to try to prove yourself powerful in ministry.

Subtly, but surely, the temptation moves us from focus on the Father to focus on proving our spiritual authority. We begin to need to pray "bigger" prayers, preach more amazing sermons, see more miracles. Soon, the need to see the spectacular becomes the focus. The emphasis is drawn away from the Father and simple, secure obedience to His will to our performance and the need to prove we are His heirs.

At this point in the wilderness Satan challenges Jesus to, "throw yourself down..." vs. 4:6, off the Temple and he gives Him a "scriptural" reason: "It is written, 'He will command his angels concerning you!'" Whenever we are tempted in the spiritual/religious arena of life, Satan will help us along with a scripture of his choosing. He helps us justify our insecurity by making us believe we are really doing this for God. *This is really not about proving my spirituality,* we think, *this is giving God the chance to prove Himself.* But that is the point; God does not need to prove Himself!

Now Jesus responds with His own scripture, "It is written: 'Do not put the Lord your God to the test.'" Jesus knew that He was not on earth to defend His Father, but to obey Him, carry out His will, demonstrate who the Father is. It was not His role to create difficult circumstances for God to then prove His power or faithfulness. Jesus was not here to test and prove God but to serve Him.

Common To All: Identity

For anyone called to follow Jesus these are basic and common temptations. In insecurity we begin to doubt what the Father has already said is true – that we are accepted as heirs of His Kingdom. When we doubt that position, the enemy moves us into striving for demonstrable proof. "If you are a child of God, heal that baby, heal your body, see that money come in, etc. If you are an heir of God's Kingdom take this risk, do this impossible thing, prove this scripture," the enemy taunts. The key to discovering the enemy's devices is not found in questioning God's ability to actually do any given thing we might ask, the key is in the word *if.* "If you are the Son of God..." It is an identity question. Who are you? And if Satan discovers that we do not accept or grasp God's embracing of us as His heirs, acceptable in His sight because of His grace extended, then Satan has found fertile ground for temptation and deception.

Jesus *knew* who He was. When the Father spoke at His baptism, "This is my Son, whom I love; with Him I am well pleased," Matt. 3:17, Jesus believed the Father. For the Son of God, the identity question was settled. Seeing this, Satan moves on to the next temptation.

Temptation Three: Right Identity, Right Vision, Wrong Strategy!

Round three is a shift in the enemy's strategy. When Satan discovers one temptation is not working in our life then he will try another. "Again, the devil took him to a very high mountain and showed him all the kingdoms of the world and their splendor," vs. 4:8. This is a very different setting. First, Satan tempted Jesus through physical hunger and need. Then he tempted Him with religious desires, and now, with the nations. This reminds me of the picture that John describes in Revelation where Jesus, restored to His throne, has the glory of all the nations paraded before Him.[3]

Satan shows Jesus a vision. He sees all the nations in all their splendor. What a sight that must have been. The enemy must have thought that this surely would lure the Son of God. Wanting the riches of the nations and the power that they represented was not Christ's temptation. The essence of this temptation is found in these words, "All this I will give you...if you will bow down and worship me."

Here is the strange thing: the nations and all their splendor already belong to Jesus. They are His rightful inheritance and the Father has assured Him they are His. So what is the temptation? What is Satan offering? This is not an identity question; Jesus knows He is the Son of God. This is not a question of misguided direction; the nations and their splendor are His. It is the right position and the right vision. What then is the temptation?

Wrong method! The enemy says, "All right! You know who you are. You know you don't need to prove it and you know what belongs to you. I will make you a better offer than the Father. I will give you the nations... now!" No waiting, no ridicule, no opposition, no trial, no jail, no beating, no cross, no death. Jesus can go straight from the quiet life of a carpenter to ruler of the universe. All He has to do to simplify the cost of obtaining His vision is change His allegiance from the Father's method to Satan's method. Whom will He obey? "Bow down and worship me," vs. 4:9, Satan says.

---

3. *Revelation 7:9-10; 21:26*

We Are The Largest Church In History

Is it possible that at strategic moments in church history, this third temptation has delayed God's purposes in the nations? Did the crusaders grasp their identity in Christ and the vision of the nations, but pollute God's purposes by bowing to a "power" methodology? Did they embrace the vision of God and the strategy of the enemy, the sword rather than the servant heart of Jesus? As we look over the historic landscape of the church, trying to grapple with the mandate to "disciple all nations," is it possible that this last temptation has been our greatest hindrance?

Jesus is unwilling to be swayed and He rebukes His enemy by name for the first time. "Away from me, Satan! For it is written: 'Worship the Lord your God, and serve him only!'" vs. 4:10. I wonder if Jesus knew for sure that He was dialoguing directly with Satan prior to the last temptation? We often interpret Jesus' life as though He had the benefit of reading the books as we have. It was the Spirit who led Him into the wilderness. Does he think the first two temptations are from the Spirit? We don't know. Jesus does not respond by name in the first two temptations. But we do know that Jesus clearly identifies whom He is speaking to when a painless, fast, and easy road to the vision of nations based on a simple shift in allegiance of power is proposed. Jesus is dealing with Lucifer himself.

What can we learn from this important season in Jesus' life as we contemplate our desire to disciple the nations? First, identity will be a struggle for the body of Christ. Who are we to talk about building nations in the face of such physical need, hunger, poverty, and disease? Who are we, and what do we hope to accomplish in the nations if we cannot perform the simplest of miraculous feats? Finally, the subtlest of all temptations, the fast, painless, power strategy to inherit the goal?

I worked in Washington, D.C. for several years. Christian groups were coming en masse with a renewed vision for discipling America. The "power" of this capital city was and is tangible. As new people arrived in the city you could see the environment begin to work on them. Whether they were politicians, activists, lobbyists, Christian or not, the shift from "national service" to "national power" as an objective was dramatic. I saw few who were able to resist the temptation.

When we study the lives of Daniel, Esther, and Joseph, men and women who greatly influenced nations, we are studying slaves and servants. God used them in their weakness. From their servant positions they gained greatness for the Kingdom of God.

The Jesus strategy is always a servant strategy!

CHAPTER 18
We Need Biblical Strategies:
The Servant Model

"...whoever wants to become great among you must be your servant, and whoever wants to be first must be your slave – just as the Son of Man did not come to be served, but to serve, and to give his life as a ransom for many."

Matthew 20:26-28

The word servant and its derivatives take up nearly five pages of listings in my NIV concordance. The men and women God used for great influence in the Kingdom were seldom people of status and power. Noah, a farmer. Abraham, an old man with a barren wife. Joseph, the youngest and despised son of herders. Moses, raised in and surrounded by power and splendor, but not of great use to God until he had lived for 40 years as an outcast and fugitive in the desert. David, the son no one remembered; a family outcast. Esther, a destitute orphan refugee with no social status or means. Ruth, a widowed refugee with a penniless mother-in-law. Nehemiah, a slave-servant to a pagan king. Daniel, the exiled boy with no means or freedom. If we are going to disciple our communities we need a fresh revelation from God on the power of serving.

The pattern continues in the New Testament as the Son of God comes to us, not as the King of the Cosmos in all His splendor and glory, but a lowly carpenter in a modest family from an insignificant village. Jesus chose ordinary working-class men to lay the foundation of the Church. And the architect of evangelism, Paul, a man of great means, status, and education is reduced to a servant of all before He can be used to build the Kingdom.

What are we to understand from this consistent scriptural theme? What is God's perspective of power that makes the humanly powerless more influential than those with great worldly status? What is this fixation Jesus has on using the smallest, the youngest, the poorest and the most disenfranchised? What does God know about power that we are still missing?

A Strategy Of Saturation

The pastor of a West African president who desired to see his poverty-stricken nation discipled by the Word of God asked me an incredibly insightful question. As we discussed national strategy for his country, he said, "If you had to choose, which would be your priority; to target the leaders of vocations in our country or to target the churches and the pastors as a strategy of national reformation?" I looked at him with great respect because so few know enough about the Kingdom to realize how key this question is. This man had done His homework with God. The Holy Spirit had helped him realize the importance of this question.

I responded that I would rather not choose, that I believed that God would build His Kingdom in every direction given the opportunity. But he prevailed in this fictional scenario, and for discussion's sake I had to choose. My response was unequivocal then. I would choose a grass roots, local church, saturation scenario for national change.

Gandhi is noted to have said that the British would rule India as long as the Indian people wanted them to. By shear force of numbers a people united in anything will over rule the power of a few at the top. The few can only be the majority influence as long as the many do not care or remain silent.

In Genesis chapter 1, God gives the human race His pre-fall mandate to "Be fruitful and increase in number; fill the earth and subdue it." This mandate was not for one man, Adam, to have authority over everything else, but for all God's human creation to saturate the earth with the knowledge of God revealed though all dimensions of everyday life. The Kingdom of God is a saturation strategy.

This is dramatically demonstrated in God's exhortation for Israel not to choose a King but rather a more grass roots system of tribal leaders and representation. Though God reasons with Israel through the prophet Samuel, they choose a King anyway.[1] God works with them in their choice to

---

1. *1 Samuel 8:19-22*

make the best of it. As Israel grows in strength politically and economically it begins to appear God has either made a mistake or reversed His opinion on power. Under Solomon's rule, Israel reaches a pinnacle of national development. Surely this strategy of a king is blessed. The ark is returned. The Temple is built. They have peace on their borders. The economy is booming. The Law is revered in the palace. What could be better?

Did God make a mistake? Was it better to have a king? The answer to that question is just one king away: Rehoboam. In one generation, one rotten egg spoils the pot. Rehoboam turns against God and destroys 300 years of development that they never again achieve. When only the kings knew the law, the people could be lead anywhere. The only protection for a nation is a people saturated with the knowledge of God and embracing responsibility.

Gandhi had a profoundly biblical point to make about power: it resides in the people. The quality of the people will ultimately determine the quality of a nation. The top levels of society can be godly or pagan, but the people determine how long their influence will last and how deep it will go. The top echelons of society can open and close doors. They can institutionalize values and principles that outlive them, but, ultimately, the saturation of those values and principles into everyday life will determine the quality of the culture.

The Kingdom Is Within You

Both the Old and the New Testament emphasize this internalized quality of the Kingdom. It is *living* the Kingdom, *being* the Kingdom that will ultimately accomplish God's mandate. In Deuteronomy, Moses passionately exhorts the people that God's law is not far from them, that they have to send messengers to bring it back from across the sea or heavens.[2] The law is with them. It is their knowing and practicing of the law that matters. The Kings should know and read the law, yes, but emphasized even more is that parents know the law and constantly teach their children to integrate it into their daily lives.

Jesus reduces all of the law into two sentences that capture the whole: "'Love the Lord your God with all your heart and with all your soul and

---

2. *Deuteronomy 30:11-14*

with all your mind.' This is the first and the greatest commandment. And the second is like it: 'Love your neighbor as yourself.'[3] This deeply personal summation embodies God's strategy. We are to be the Kingdom. We are to live the Kingdom. The salt and light of our lives, whether we lead or serve, will "salt and light" the earth with the knowledge of God. You and I are God's strategy. Discipleship, or learning to apply God's thinking to our daily lives, is God's focus.

As I began to realize this personally, I longed to live in a "neighborhood" to understand how this worked itself out practically. I had discipled students and leaders in their professions for years, and I would continue, but what did the neighbor mandate look like? Was I in danger of knowing God's message, but missing His strategy?

I bought a home in the southern part of the U.S.A. on a street of 14 houses. I chose a multi-ethnic street because God loves the nations. I got a little house because I am single and travel extensively. God is a good steward of resources. I began to work on my yard, neglected for at least a decade, because God loves beauty and we are to value the material things He gives us. In the first weeks, my neighbors would watch me as they worked in their yards. I would wave and keep on trimming, raking, hauling. After a time, some started to come by when they saw me out working. They would say how nice the house looked and ask my name. We'd talk gardening for a few minutes and they'd be gone. Jesus is interested in what we are interested in and has given plants to us to steward. I would go in the house and write their names down so I would remember, because God knows our names. After more time our "yard conversations" would get past the weather and the trees to what I do. Finding out I was a missionary didn't lead to much discussion because it was so foreign to them, but we continued to get to know each other through the things we had in common: houses, yards, plants, neighborhood safety, etc.

As I worked on my home, I prayed for my neighbors, their families, our neighborhood. About six months after I moved in, one neighbor made a beeline for me one morning. He said, "My wife's sister just died. Please pray for her." Within a week the husband next door saw me in my yard and made a direct path to me and said, "My wife said her job is more important than me and I'm afraid I'm going to lose her. Please pray." I was

---

3. *Matthew 22:37-40*

astounded. We had never spoken of prayer. We had hardly said anything about God. They knew I was in ministry overseas, but we had not shared any details. Where did this desire for God in me come from, this trust with the most intimate pain in their lives? I can only believe it was the testimony of my yard work and neighborly concern. They saw Jesus in the care of the yard, house, the desire to know and remember each of their names, the willingness to be "one of them" first, the shared concern for all of our homes, families and safety. They saw Jesus in my life and they wanted more of Him in their crisis.

Our Message Will Never Have More Authority Than Our Life

One of my early influences in the Kingdom used to emphasize that in the Christian faith, you are the message. It is, in that sense, that biblical faith is not a religion or a set of ideas to talk about without application to our lives. Following Jesus is a way of life, a relationship with God that turns into the Kingdom lived out on a daily basis. I fear that, for many, following Jesus has become a religion, an ideal we can talk about believing without it necessarily changing any dimension of our lifestyle. Our faith becomes about salvation and then life after death and there is a parenthesis around the rest of our existence as though God has nothing to do with it.

It is interesting that Christians have no difficulty talking about *how* Jesus would have lived as a carpenter those first thirty years. They know that He would have been timely in His work; He would have treated His workers and customers respectfully and cared for them as people; He would have paid His bills on time. We understand that if Jesus made a bookshelf, the shelves would be straight, the construction sturdy, and it would be beautiful, even if simple. He loved quality. Jesus would have taken good care of His tools and He would not have wasted wood and other materials. There is this innate understanding in all of us that He would have been generous with His income, mowed his lawn if He had one and that His house would have been clean. Jesus' personal hygiene would have been exemplary. And, if we push our thinking a little harder, we know why Jesus would have lived like this...because of who His Father was.

The testimony of Jesus' personal life for thirty years in Nazareth was the authority base of His three years of ministry. If we cannot serve our family with the principles of the Kingdom, if we cannot serve our neighbors with the principles of the Kingdom, how can we serve the nations with Kingdom values? I have to go one step further in this and wonder – if every Christian in the world were living their personal life by the values of the Kingdom, would the nations then *be* discipled?

The Kingdom Of Light: Service Not Control

The Kingdom of Light is service. The Kingdom of Darkness is control. It is that simple! If our discipleship strategies are power-based they will fail. The system of the world is based in power – let's take over and make it better. The Kingdom of God is service-based. Had it been better for Jesus to come with earthly trappings of power, He would have. If control from the top worked, all of Eastern Europe would actually be communist. Leaders may serve the people into change, but ultimately, if a nation is not changed on a personal level, it is not discipled. God's values may be written into the civil statutes of a nation and that will have an effect, but if the culture is to be changed those same values must also be written onto the hearts of the people.

I have to think that calling service in government *civil service* must have come from scripture. The power of the position is in the service to the people. In the last half-century we have begun to think that we can help create democratic nations through military action from outside forces. We certainly can change a regime by force. However, changing the hearts and minds of the people is another matter. The thinking that created the problem cannot fix the problem and, ultimately, the community will and must be changed, the Kingdom built – one individual at a time.

CHAPTER 19
We Need a Godly Perspective on Change

"You know how to interpret the appearance of the sky, but you cannot interpret the signs of the times."

Matthew 16:3

"Men of Issachar, who understood the times and knew what Israel should do..."

1 Chronicles 12:32

If we are going to have influence in the nations, like the men of Issachar, we must be people who know the signs of our times.

As we talked about in chapter eight, until the 1500's the earth was definitely flat, according to the experts. Explorers and navigators held the view that sailing to the edges of the world meant certain death. Falling over the edge of livable surface meant slipping into the "other world" of demons and dragons. Maps of the era are suitably frightening. Had this dogma gone unquestioned, Columbus would have stayed home.

The "flat earth" hypothesis was not only the scientific view of the planet, but the theological view of the day as well. A flat earth was central to the doctrinal view of heaven and hell. The church held that man was the center of God's universe; heaven was up and hell was down. The application of this truth was the conclusion that the earth must be flat. In the absence of more information, everyone agreed.

The first scientists who challenged this idea where brutally treated, some executed by the church. They were not only viewed as wrong scientifically, but were deemed heretical for challenging God's Word and authority.

In this case, however, the church and the traditional Christian view of the day were wrong and the scientists were right. The earth is not flat, but more spherical and as we discovered more about the universe, rotating planets, and gravity, up and down became more figurative language than concrete in our perceptions.

What of heaven and hell then? Man's centrality to God's creation? Was God's Word in danger of being discredited, even disproved, by science and research? In the 1540's they were afraid that might be the case. But it was not. Only man's understanding of what God meant in His Word has changed. Man is the center of God's creation, but not necessarily geographically. Heaven and Hell are both clearly revealed truths, but their exact location is still a mystery.

The God who created all, sees all, knows all infinitely, is not shaken when our limited understanding goes through a learning curve. His supreme desire is that we ever grow to be more like Him. As the old hymn declares, "He is changing me," and our view of His creation. God is not in conflict with truth, with facts, or any reality of the seen or unseen world, and He is not afraid of change.

Everything Is Changing!

In our age, it seems everything is changing constantly. After the year 2000, it is estimated that the average person will change professions four to five times in his/her working lifetime. Engineers today find that half their professional knowledge is obsolete every five years. Graduates today have been exposed to more information in one year than their grandparents were in a lifetime. Ninety percent of the information and knowledge required in the next five years has yet to be invented. Mind boggling, isn't it? To us perhaps, but not to God.

God is not experiencing a knowledge surge. He has had all this in His grasp from the beginning. We have nothing to fear from information and knowledge, old or new. For the facts can only reveal God, His nature and His ways.[1] But, as finite human beings, we do fear change and always have.

---

1. *Roman 1:12*

Fear Not!

Imagine yourself as an Israelite in Moses' day. Your people have lived in Egypt for 400 years. For 300 years, you have been slaves to the pharaohs. In the last few months you have left Egypt and all that is known to you and your people. You are in the middle of a desert; you have no known source of food and water; you cannot go back to Egypt; you have no idea what is ahead in this unseen Promised Land. You are experiencing a paradigm change of all you know and God must remind you time and time again, "Fear not," for He is with you.

Today, we experience that kind of shaking change, again and again, in one lifetime. In a world daily attuned by microchips, global economics, Hubble telescopes and instant information, our sense of reality can get shaky. When our reality begins to unravel we get insecure and, often, insecurity results in rigidity and a desire to control. When we shut down and refuse to understand the changes in our world, we stop growing. The fruit of all this fear is that we miss God's expanding revelation of Himself through the universe He created.

Esther came to understand that God had a plan for her nation in the crisis in her life. She realized that her Uncle Mordecai's words were true, "Who knows but that you have come to the royal position for such a time as this?"[2] The pressures and changes of her day were purposeful for the Kingdom of God. She was afraid, but she turned to God in her fear and saw change work for His glory in her people.

In this day of global upheaval and what feels like disaster and doom, we need an Uncle Mordecai to tell us that our times are purposeful. For, if God tarries and the end of the world is not at hand, we may live in a century of the greatest influence on the world for God's Kingdom in the history of the human race. Let's get God's perspective on our times.

Global Social Revolution

One simple way of looking at the evolution of human societies and cultures is to see it in three primary cycles: the tribal or feudal system, the great city-states, and our more modern concept of nations.

---

2. *Esther 4:14*

The Feudal System

Virtually all of human society was, at one time, organized around something resembling a tribe. Whether the leaders were patriarchs, chiefs, or landlords, communities were organized and defined around the availability and ownership of land. In Europe, this was called the feudal system. The head of this socio/economic system was the landlord. The landlord owned the land and the peasants worked it. The landlord provided any education, healthcare, or law. In practice, a farm or a farm-based village defined citizenship and community. Itinerant priests traveled from farm to farm. The landlord recruited, trained, and equipped the military. Early European monarchs depended on the benevolent support of this landlord's armies. During one century or another, virtually every region of the world was organized in these tribal entities. Many in Africa and Middle East nations are still tribal underneath the veneer of more modern social structures. This "tribal" age is the age of Abraham through the era of the Judges of Israel in scripture. Until King Saul, Israel was a consortium of 12 tribal peoples loosely networked through the leadership of a judge.

The Great City States

Population-driven cultural evolution took its course and, in one way or another, the earth's communities were transformed. The next period of social structure was characterized by the development of the great city-states such as Rome, Athens, Alexandria, Constantinople, Babylon, Hamburg, Paris. These cosmopolitan centers became the way we defined nation. One was a citizen of Rome. Rome built the roads, was the seat of education, controlled the economy. Taxes were paid to and collected by Rome. This is the world of Paul's day. Paul held citizenship in Rome and in Jerusalem, dual citizenship he found useful in his work for the Kingdom. Had we lived in this era, our world-view would have us define nations as city/states.

Populations continued to grow and finally outgrew the political/economic infrastructure of city/states. Rome and systems like it became incapable of meeting the needs of their constituents and outgrew their ability to be governed and organized in this way. The world order of nations began to turn itself over once again. Today, none of us have our citizenship in a city/state or even really comprehend a world organized in this way.

Modern Nations

Today we speak of Italy, with a capitol in Rome, of Greece with a city called Athens. We understand that Hamburg is in Germany and Constantinople in Turkey, Alexandria in Egypt and Paris in France. Geopolitical borders have been created, modified, and changed again and again to form the world we understand in our time.

If you and I were asked where we are from internationally we would name our nation. Even if our nation still has tribes we would identify ourselves by our nation first. We carry national passports and discuss national economies and educational systems. We sing national anthems and fly our national flag. We have national constitutions and national governments and tend to see our culture as defined by national tastes and values. This is the mindset of our times. We tend to view this as the way nations should be, forgetting that this was not the concept when God spoke to Abraham about making him a nation. Nor was it the concept when Jesus told us to go to all nations. And yet all of scripture is telling us to address the needs of and disciple all nations.

Here We Go Again!

Population is again driving change in our geopolitical structures and economies. Increasingly today with nearly zero population growth in Europe, a bursting population in Asia, and inadequate population-to-resources equations in other regions, our world is once again evolving in how we define ourselves. National economies are failing or becoming unstable. National militaries are finding themselves inadequate to protect. National education systems do not prepare a generation for the global community in which we live. And for perhaps the fourth time in human history, society and nations as we know them are reinventing themselves!

Europe leads the way in this with the formation of the European Union. It's not that the French, German, English, Spanish, and others do not love their nations, cultures, languages, and even currencies. They do. But their systems no longer work for the populations in our world today. They must redesign themselves to fit the reality of the 21st Century. And Europe is not alone. As soon as the European Union begins to take shape one hears discussions of "The Americas" with new treaties and economic dialogue between North and South America. A new phrase appears in our vocabulary, "Australasia." We see new collaboration and coordination in the Middle East and identify it as the "Arab World." We talk of global economies, regional stability, peace, multinational forces, and even world courts.

In the face of this dramatic shift many people panic, forgetting that it has all happened before. Some begin to focus on the end of the world and one world government instead of understanding that every major shift in history has moved us in that direction. But the church's job remains the same: disciple all nations. History can give us a more positive understanding of global change and the times we live in. We are not the first generation of believers to face global shifts in social systems. And, if God tarries, we may not be the last.

Change Is God's Catalyst

Change is not always cataclysmic but it is always a catalyst. History teaches us at least three wonderful truths about change:

1. Whatever God meant by nations in Genesis, He intended His truth to be applicable to all times and all nations, regardless of change.
2. Throughout history, great change has provided the best climate for influence.
3. The church has, in some measure, found its voice and brought God's truth to influence each major shift in our global history.

In this century where, by God's grace, we have the largest population of believers worldwide in the history of man, and we are in what could be one of the greatest centuries of change in the history of the planet, will the body of Christ have a voice? In an age of change, Calvin gave us a concept of public education, Wilberforce pushed for just labor practices and laws, Carey for economic development; others founded the Red Cross, developed a code of ethics for treating prisoners of war, rules of war, scientific research, laws of evidence, and the list can go on.

These things took place where men and women of God understood that we couldn't control change, but we can use it. We can steer change towards the values and principles of God.

All over the world leaders are scrambling to find new definitions of just wars, just rules of war, legal combatants, protocol of prisons, labor laws for women and children, women's rights, the rights of multicultural populations, religious freedom, the poor versus the rich, the power of governance, balance of powers, national versus international issues. We are panicked with the sheer volume and totality of change we see. God is not! And none of these issues are new; they have all been dealt with before. And God dealt with them all in discipling Israel, complete with a record of the values that are not negotiable if we want quality of life, and volumes of case studies of success and failure.

What if the largest church in history linked up with the greatest community-building values in history to bring the greatest Kingdom revolution in history?

Let The Enemy Have His Convention In A Phone Booth

Who's to say when the end of the world will come? For two thousand years, believers have thought it would be in their lifetime, including the apostles who walked with Jesus. But it was not in their lifetime, or century, or their millennium. The end of the world as we know it will come. But Jesus tells us not to focus on that, but rather to be salt and light in our times, to work until He comes. If we had believed that and discipled the evangelized nations in the last 150 years, we would have transformed Southern Africa, America, Brazil, Argentina, Chile...*and we still can!*

What are we waiting for? We may be living in the greatest century in Church history, if:

- We grasp the whole God of the whole Bible.
- We grasp God's commitment to the whole community and all nations.
- We ignore our fear of change and embrace these times as the greatest for potential Kingdom impact.
- We stop staring at the influence of evil and give ourselves wholeheartedly to the influence of good.

Who's to say if we, the body of Christ, did our jobs with God's thinking, that the enemy of our God could not have "his convention in a phone booth?"

ADDENDUM
&
BIBLIOGRAPHY

The OLD TESTAMENT TEMPLATE

ADDENDUM I
The Bible's Table Of Contents:
God's Big Picture

For an entire year I studied the Bible and its Table of Contents from the standpoint of God's purposes in it. Making the assumption God did inspire each of the books of the Bible, and that the Church Fathers were inspired with the ordering of these same books, and assuming that it is no small miracle that the church has basically agreed on these things for the last 2000 years, then what was God's strategy and emphasis in the books chosen and the order in which they are placed? This was a mind-blowing study!

OVERVIEW

First, we have the five books of Moses, the template of Hebrew thought.

Genesis: The origins of the cosmos, individual, family, tribe, and nation, and, of course, sin.

Exodus: Israel's current events from God's perspective and what God is doing with Israel as a community in space and time.

Leviticus: The formation and workings of the priesthood and the tabernacle.

Numbers: The logistics of discipling these people into a nation.

Deuteronomy: The overview of how God wanted Israel to live in every area of life. These five books, the Pentateuch, laid the foundation for all of the Old Testament and, as we will see, for the New Testament as well.

ALL REFER BACK TO MOSES

Every other book in the Old Testament refers back to these first five books. They evaluate the history and forecast the future of Israel based on what God has lain down in the Law. The rest of the Old Testament relays events and history based on the answer to one simple question: "Are we living up to God's principles in the first five books?"

Let's look at what God emphasizes in the Table of Contents of the Bible.

Joshua: Community-Government
How they do in the Promised Land in the first generation of political action.

Judges: Community-Government
How the next 13 generations of Judges do in the political arena.

Ruth: Individual-Family
After seven books emphasizing communities and nations, God narrows in on two powerless and poor women who are blessed when they obey in faithfulness.

1 and 2 Samuel, 1 and 2 Kings, and 1 and 2 Chronicles: Community-Government
The history of the political leaders and how they did or didn't obey God's law.

That makes eight books for Government, one for Family, one for the Priesthood, twelve books for Community, and one for the Individual. Seeing any pattern yet?

Ezra, Nehemiah, and Esther are a trilogy. They are not in order. Esther is actually first chronologically, Ezra second, and Nehemiah third. They are all exiles in the Capitol city of Sousa. In about 479 B.C. Esther marries King Xerxes and as a result is used of God to save the lives of all the Jewish people in exile. In about 456 B.C., 21 years after Esther's book, Ezra, who is a priest, returns to Jerusalem and rebuilds the temple, but the city is still in chaos and disrepair. He is there 13 years but without success in restoring the community when a letter reaches Nehemiah, part of the King's palace security guard, telling of the disasters in Jerusalem. Nehemiah is sent by the King with supplies and support to rebuild the wall and restore order and infrastructure to the community. So we have:

Ezra: Community-Priesthood
Nehemiah: Community-Government
Esther: Community-Family and Government

Esther saves the people. Ezra restores the temple and the Law, and Nehemiah rebuilds the government and community economic system – all areas emphasized by God as essential parts of Kingdom life.

Our count is now Government ten, Family two, Ecclesiastical order two, fifteen books that emphasize Community and one that emphasizes the Individual.

What Is Job Doing Here?

Job: Individual-Family

Job is the oldest book of the Bible to the best of our understanding. He was, perhaps, a contemporary of Abraham. I think most of us see the wisdom of the Church Fathers in not selecting Job as the first book of the Bible. Its theme of suffering and personal warfare is tough stuff for the most mature believer. However, Job is the second book in the scriptures to look at the story of an individual without it being particularly important to the history of the community. Like Ruth, Job is important because of his walk of faith and obedience to God under great duress. Job begins with great power, but is reduced to nothing by a series of attacks and disasters. After seventeen books of God focusing on the principles by which He has made the universe to work, the blessing of knowing and applying these truths to our lives, and the curse of not obeying them, a quite different focus is introduced in Job. For the first time since Genesis, God tells us that there are additional challenges to obedience. We have an enemy and, even having made all the right choices, there may be another explanation for difficult circumstances in our life. We may be experiencing Satan's attack! Today, we seem to have reversed this emphasis to everything being a spiritual attack and almost nothing the result of our choices.

The Wisdom Literature

We love the quartet of wisdom literature, perhaps, because each book focuses on the individual. While written by kings these books primarily deal with different dimensions of the believer's personal life. What is important in our daily lives? Worship? Wisdom? Work? Family? All of them!

Psalms: Individual and Worship
Proverbs: Individual and Wisdom
Ecclesiastes: Individual and Work
Song of Songs: Individual and the Wedding (Family)
That brings us to ten books focused on Government, three on Family
six on the Individual, and two on the Priesthood or Ecclesiastical order.

The Prophets

Then we come to the 17 prophets. Some authors of these books were
priests; some were shepherds, some government officials. However, they
all speak to nations or communities as a whole. They all emphasize the
"cause and effect" nature of our choices and the resulting blessing or
curse. Each prophet focuses on four major areas of sin no matter what
nations they are addressing:
Idolatry: Ecclesiastical order
Political Justice: Government
Immorality: Family and individual
Economic Injustice: Business and finance
God's emphasis on the importance of the Ecclesiastical institution, or
church, Government, the Individual, and the Family is overwhelming.
The focus on the community is almost unanimous and the emphasis on
knowing God's thinking and aligning ourselves with it in how we live is
complete.

The New Testament

What do we see in the New Testament? Each Gospel writer empha-
sizes a different source of authenticity:
Matthew defends Jesus as the messiah by drawing heavily from the
Old Testament sources: the **ecclesiastical history.**
Mark emphasizes Jesus' relationship with the material word and His
power over it: **science.**
Luke takes the view of an investigator looking at the testimony of
those who were with Jesus: **legal.**

John uses the personal, eyewitness account of the individual.

The Gospels, like the books of Moses, lay a holistic foundation for the Lordship of Christ. Moses lays a holistic basis for God's rule over all of Creation and life; the Apostles lay the same foundation for the Lordship of Christ.

Now we come to the book of **Acts,** which I think could be called "The Explosion!" If Acts were the only book to guide us in our work, for the Kingdom, we could be quite comfortable with our ministry in the last century. The word about Christ bursts out from the new church and explodes with conversions, gifts of the Holy Spirit, healing, miracles, persecution, public proclamation in Jerusalem and beyond, and the establishing of the church internationally. The "explosion" begins with the new converts accused of being drunk and ends with some of them in jail. What a roller coaster.

In the books that follow, we begin to see, and deal with, some of the issues within this new international church movement. As the gospel travels out of Jewish territory and begins to encounter the surrounding worldviews, and a shifting emphasis amongst the Jews as well, Romans ask the question, "What are we going to do with the Old Testament?" 1 Corinthians takes up the question of how the Holy Spirit works. In 2 Corinthians they ask where the authority of this new church comes from.

The next 19 letters reveal a pattern of themes not dissimilar to the Old Testament. In various circumstances, nations, churches, and in individual lives we begin to deal with the drift hazards of the new church. What are some of the major themes of these letters and issues?

1. What do we do with the Old Testament and the laws of Moses?
2. What is the function of this Holy Spirit?
3. Where does authority come from in this new Church?
4. How do you/we know you/we have authority?
5. What are the conditions for elders and deacons and the character of a church leader?
6. How do we discern false teaching from true?
7. Questions of how we live and our position on family, immorality, government, finances, honesty, work and generosity.
8. The nature of eternity and life after death.

9. Perspectives on persecution and endurance.

10. The supremacy and return of Christ.

11. The end of time.

You can almost feel the struggle of the New Testament leaders trying to integrate the Old and the New, between the church slipping towards the Law or towards the Spirit. Throughout all these discussions, Christ is presented as the only way to salvation, the Law and the prophets as the teachers of how we should live, and the Spirit as the one who leads us into applying the principles of the Law into daily life. Nowhere do we see one discarded in preference of the other. All of the books are full of the tension from integrating the Old Testament with the New Testament.

What Does Jesus Say About All Of This:

Matthew is the first gospel, I believe, for a reason. Matthew makes an all out effort to link the life and teaching of Jesus with the Old Testament. At least 49 times in 28 chapters Matthew links the teaching and life of Jesus with Moses and the prophets. In Matthew 5, Jesus makes His position clear on the place of the Law.

Matthew 5:17-19

17 Do not think that I have come to abolish the Law or the Prophets; I have not come to abolish them but to fulfill them.

18 I tell you the truth, until heaven and earth disappear, not the smallest letter, not the least stroke of a pen, will by any means disappear from the Law until everything is accomplished.

19 Anyone who breaks one of the least of these commandments and teaches others to do the same will be called least in the kingdom of heaven, but whoever practices and teaches these commands will be called great in the kingdom of heaven.

This is such an amazing passage. Jesus makes it clear that the new messages of forgiveness and salvation on their own are not adequate for discipleship, but rather build on the foundation of the Law and the prophets. In Matthew 13:52, Jesus says, "Every teacher of religious law who has become a disciple in the Kingdom of Heaven is like a person who brings out of the storehouse the new teaching as well as the old." In Matthew 5:19 Jesus exhorts that the teaching of the new without the foundations of the old will produce weakness and the "least" in the Kingdom, but combining the two will produce greatness in the Kingdom of God. Mark 7:8-13 accuses the Pharisees of substituting God's laws with their own traditions. And in Luke 16:16-17 Jesus challenges the crowds that by preaching the Good News of the Kingdom He does not mean that the law has lost its force; the law is stronger and more lasting than the universe itself.

After Jesus clarifies the place of the Law and the prophets in Matthew 5, He goes on to give six examples of how He builds His teaching on the teaching of Moses:

Do not murder: Jesus affirms the commandment that "Thou shalt not kill," but He goes further to build on that law. He says that now that the Spirit is coming we should not even act in anger. In fact, we should go a step farther and be reconciled before we come to worship. In other words, even though we are saved and forgiven we are not to murder and, if we are saved, our standard will be even higher.

Do not commit adultery: Jesus agrees that Moses taught that they were not to commit adultery, but He is challenging them to an even higher standard of a pure heart.

Divorce: Moses taught them that divorce must be legally carried out, but Jesus is telling them that it must be under the direst circumstances or it is equal to adultery itself.

Be Truthful: Moses taught them to not break an oath; Jesus goes a step farther to say that they are not to break a promise or a verbal commitment.

Righteous vengeance: Moses taught that they should only seek righteous vengeance, but Jesus says to give up the right to personal vengeance altogether.

Love your neighbor: Moses encouraged them to love their neighbor; Jesus says do that and go much farther – love your enemy.

What Happens If We Do Not Lay The Foundation?

What happens when we remove the foundational principles of the Old Testament in our discipleship of new Christians? Is it possible that we produce a Rwanda where a church with sixty-plus years of constant revival can participate in tribal genocide? Is it possible that we produce an American church where recent Gallup polls say there is no measurable difference between the lifestyle of the Christian population and that of the non-Christian? Is it possible that this is the reason divorce in the Bible Belt of the U.S.A. now exceeds the divorce rate in the rest of America? Can this be why the average Christian businessman in Korea is no more committed to his word in a contract than the average non-Christian businessman? Could this be why in 80 percent converted Nagaland, 70 percent of the teens in the capital are reported to be drug addicts. Is it possible that this is why modern Christianity makes no measurable difference in the landscape of the societies that surround us? Are we preaching a gospel that, because it is not grounded in the Old Testament teachings, is producing the "least in the Kingdom of heaven?"

When we preach what Paul calls the "milk of the gospel" – salvation, repentance, heaven and hell, and the forgiveness of sin – without the "meat" of how Christ expects us to live, we are in danger of producing a new mysticism, a religious belief detached from any physical reality in a life. We develop a faith that requires no change in thinking or lifestyle that is unattached to the cause and effect relationship of our choices and the laws of God. We are called to "take every thought captive" and to be "conformed to the mind of Christ." We are to be "transformed by the renewing of our minds." How can we do this if we have not laid the same foundations Jesus laid? Jesus was discipled by the Old Testament. Paul was discipled from the Old Testament. We do not understand their thinking if we are not interpreting the New in light of the Old.[1]

In the face of a world lost in sin, Jesus had time to simply live out the witness of the principles of God in daily life in the context of His family, work, and community. Less than 10 percent of His entire life was spent in direct ministry and open proclamation of the gospel. He spent ten times more of His life living it out. His authority in ministry was, in part, the authority of His life in applying Moses and the prophets to His times.

---

1. *1 Corinthians 3:2; 2 Corinthians 10:5; Hebrews 5:12-14; Romans 12:2*

We Do Have Time

Is it possible that we have bought into an eschatological anxiousness that keeps us from doing the whole work of discipleship? The great reformer Luther was asked what he would do today if he knew Jesus was coming back tomorrow? His reply was that he would plant the fruit tree he had planned yesterday to plant tomorrow, because Jesus said to "tarry" until He comes.[2] The Amplified translation says to "occupy (do business with) until I come." A word search in the Greek: tarry (pragmateuomoi: To busy oneself with, to do business, to trade.) Kittle's Dictionary: make a profit, to deal with radically, to investigate closely, to render political service, those charged with affairs of State, of intellectual pursuits, of business affairs.

The early reformers of the first millennium and a half of church history didn't just think different things than today's believers, they thought differently about all of life. True repentance is changed thinking and Christ cannot transform us if we do not seek to hold and live out His view about all of life!

Be The Good Neighbor

In many cultures, the most important indicator of what kind of person you are and of your value is how you relate to your neighbor. This was also part of the Hebrew or biblical view of the world and the view emphasized throughout scripture and in the teaching of Jesus. He stresses this community perspective by putting our love of God alongside our being a good neighbor. He said that second in priority only to our devotion to God, is how we treat those who live around us. In Matthew 7:12, Jesus summarizes the entire Law and the prophets to mean treating others the way you would like to be treated. In Matthew 22:34-40, He said "You must love the Lord your God with all your heart, all your soul, and all your mind. This is the first and the greatest commandment. And the second is *equally* important: Love your neighbor as yourself." Loving my neighbor is as important as loving God. If I love God, I will love my neighbor!

---

2. *Luke 19:11-13*

Who Is My Neighbor

In Luke 10:26-27, a religious expert in the law tried to get a limited definition of neighbor. He asked Jesus, "and who is my neighbor?" In response to this Jesus tells the story of the Good Samaritan as an illustration. He changes the definition of neighbor from "those who live close to me" to the one who crosses your path and who is in need. In other words, anyone, everyone.

What happens when the Church switches the biblical emphasis from our responsibility to our neighbor to personal holiness? I believe we create the new monasticism, a spiritual pursuit of God that is completely alienated from social responsibility and action. We create the concept that my personal holiness is completely independent from how I interact with the community God has placed me in. I feel I can love God and have almost nothing to do with the people living around me; I can have national truth without national responsibility; I can actually seek to live with only those who believe as I do so that my life will not be sullied with the messy lives of non-Christians. Our walk with God begins to be evaluated strictly on personal merits alienated from our participation in the life of our community.

Years ago I was sponsored by a concerned Christian to attend a political fundraiser in California. My benefactor thought I might be able to get to know and influence some of the county officials. At the time, this area was one of the most Christianized communities in America. I spent quite a bit of time with a local county judge, a single woman about my age. She was very honest and forthright so I asked her why she did what she did, knowing that she had a tough job and couldn't be motivated by the money or the hours. She said that, at the end of the day, she did it to help the children at risk. She had great authority as a judge to intervene in their lives at points where it could make a big difference.

I asked her what part of the local community she found most open to help bring these children into homes. She knew that I was a Christian and she seemed reluctant to answer until I encouraged her I was not thin-skinned; I wanted an honest observation. She said, "Well, it is not the Christians who want these children." She had found the greatest openness in this evangelized county to be amongst the Jehovah Witnesses and the Mormons. The great revivals of this county in the 70's produced the first mega churches, the first contemporary Christian music, the first of a new breed of Christian bookstore, but it has still not touched the community.

President Mbeki, of South Africa, has been quoted as saying that he would be behind any effort to help change the Christian community's lack of social concern. While the ruling political party has a majority of Christians, it is the Muslim minority who has the vision to transform South Africa and is doing so.

Let's bring back the whole Kingdom with the whole Bible and the supremacy of Christ in all things!

ADDENDUM II
Things I am Not Saying!

My study and research for this material has been almost entirely from the scriptures themselves. In the very beginning of my search I felt the Lord say that I was to leave aside reformation history and books on the domains. This has worked very well for two reasons. The first is that I teach the material straight from the Bible rather than from history. This means that as I travel the nations there is no cultural or historical bias laid over the top of the material. I am not teaching some other country's interpretation in history, but the Word God left for all nations, for all times. The benefit of that cannot be over emphasized. Secondly, it allows me to be both appreciative and critical of the Church Fathers; appreciative of the great revelations they did have in their nations in their times, and the way that influenced history, but also critical of what they were missing from scripture that would have made them even more influential. This is certainly not the only way to study, but it has proved most beneficial for me.

As I have spoken on these issues worldwide, I have become more aware of the many great conflicts in the body of Christ around concepts like the Kingdom, dominion, and discipling nations. I am constantly faced with tough questions that come from a particular view as opposed to scripture itself. I am not qualified to speak to any of these views, as I have not studied any of them. But I would like to clarify what I am saying by telling you what I am not saying. For some of you this will be a waste of time; for others it may be the thing that helps you hear my message without interpreting it through some other position.

Things I Am Not Saying:

1. I am not saying that we can create heaven here on earth.
We cannot create perfection here on earth. Only when Jesus returns

and a new heaven and new earth are established will we see Him in His full glory. However, we can reveal Him in part and better our communities by living out and working for God's values in all of life.

2. I am not saying that Jesus will come back once we disciple all the nations.

Only the Father knows when Jesus will return. The date is never to be our concern; we are always to be prepared. Our job is to obey Christ until He returns, which as Luther said, means "tarry", "take dominion" until He does come. When we put the two truths together we develop a sense of urgency that works against discipleship, which takes time.

3. I am not saying that Christians are to "take over" society and tell everyone else what to do and how to live.

We will not eliminate sin in our world by discipling communities. However, we will, with evangelism and discipleship, make better communities. This, in turn, reveals God in a broader way and works for more evangelism and discipleship, which can create even better communities. But you will always have the lost and the saved who are undiscipled and they will continue to make choices that are less than godly. We are not looking for control; we are looking for influence. The way of the Kingdom is not by force but by persuasion. We are salt and light, not a hammer and sickle.

4. I am not saying that God died and left us here to do the best we can.

God is very much alive and active in our efforts. We can glean the principles from scripture with faithful study and prayer. But we cannot possibly know how to apply these principles to our nations and our times without fresh revelation in time and space from the Holy Spirit. We are not alone with God's manual; He is with us in applying the Word just as He was with Moses.

5. I am not saying we should do everything like the English, the Americans, the Swiss, the Dutch or (fill in the blank with your nationality.)

A great temptation in teaching and working with this material is to choose a particular application as the reference rather than sticking with

God's examples in scripture. When we do that our listeners immediately think of all that nation's faults and our point is lost. There is no "discipled nation" and there are no nations that do not have elements of God's principles in practice. God's goal is not for us to copy one another but to seek a dynamic equivalency of that Kingdom principle in our community, in our time, and in our way. God loves variety. We can learn from everyone. We should seek to emulate only God, not one another.

BIBLIOGRAPHY AND ADDITIONAL RESOURCES

Cahill, Thomas - *How the Irish Saved Civilization*
Nan A. Talese, Bantam Doubleday Dell Publishing Group, Inc. 1540
Broadway, New York 10036, ISBN 0-385-41849-3, 1996

Cassidy, Michael - *The Passing Summer*
Hodder & Stoughton, London. Sydney. Auckland. Toronto,
ISBN 0-340-42627-6, 1989

Kinoti, George - *Hope For Africa and What The Christian Can Do*
African Institute for Scientific Research and Development,
ISBN 9966-9922-0-0, 1994

Miller, Darrow L. – *Discipling Nations*
YWAM Publishing, P.O. Box 55787, Seattle, WA 98155,
ISBN 1-57658-015-6

Olsen, Bruce E. - *Bruchko*
Creation House Carole Strum, IL 60187
ISBN 0-88419-133-8, 1978

Ralph Mattson and Arthur Miller - *Finding A Job You Can Love*
Thomas Nelson Publishers, Nashville. Camden. New York,
ISBN 0-8407-5817-0, 1982

Schaeffer, Francis A. - *Genesis in Space and Time*
InterVarsity Press Downers, IL 60515 ISBN 0-87784-363-7, 1972

Stott, John - *Involvement: Being a Responsible Christian in a Non-Christian Society*
Fleming H. Revell Co. Old Tappan, NJ 07675,
ISBN 0-8007-1418-0, 1985

Stott, John - *New Issues Facing Christians Today*
Fleming H. Revel-Baker Book House Co. Grand Rapids, MI 49516
ISBN 0-8007-5312-7, 1990

Sheldon, Charles M. - *In His Steps*
Zondervan, ISBN 0310327512, 1984

Websites:
The London Institute of Contemporary Christianity
www.licc.org.uk

The Relationships Foundation
www.relationshipsfoundation.org

Jubilee 2000
www.jubilee2000uk.org

Professor Prabhu Guptara, Switzerland
www.prabhu.guptara.net

Vishal Mangalwadi, India
www.vishalmangalwadi.com